D0370981

The definitive
management ideas
of the year from
Harvard Business Review.

2021

HBR's 10 Must Reads series is the definitive collection of ideas and best practices for aspiring and experienced leaders alike. These books offer essential reading selected from the pages of *Harvard Business Review* on topics critical to the success of every manager.

Titles include:

HBR's 10 Must Reads 2015
HBR's 10 Must Reads 2016
HBR's 10 Must Reads 2017
HBR's 10 Must Reads 2018
HBR's 10 Must Reads 2019
HBR's 10 Must Reads 2020
HBR's 10 Must Reads for CEOs
HBR's 10 Must Reads for New Managers
HBR's 10 Must Reads on AI, Analytics, and the New Machine Age
HBR's 10 Must Reads on Boards
HBR's 10 Must Reads on Building a Great Culture
HBR's 10 Must Reads on Business Model Innovation
HBR's 10 Must Reads on Change Management
HBR's 10 Must Reads on Collaboration
HBR's 10 Must Reads on Communication
HBR's 10 Must Reads on Design Thinking
HBR's 10 Must Reads on Diversity
HBR's 10 Must Reads on Emotional Intelligence
HBR's 10 Must Reads on Entrepreneurship and Startups
HBR's 10 Must Reads on Innovation
HBR's 10 Must Reads on Leadership
HBR's 10 Must Reads on Leadership (Vol. 2)
HBR's 10 Must Reads on Leadership for Healthcare
HBR's 10 Must Reads on Leadership Lessons from Sports
HBR's 10 Must Reads on Making Smart Decisions
HBR's 10 Must Reads on Managing Across Cultures
HBR's 10 Must Reads on Managing in a Downturn

HBR'S
10
MUST
READS

The definitive
management ideas
of the year from
Harvard Business Review.

2021

HARVARD BUSINESS REVIEW PRESS

Boston, Massachusetts

Library of Congress Cataloging-in-Publication Data

Names: Harvard Business Review Press.
Title: HBR's 10 must reads 2021 : the definitive management ideas of the
    year from Harvard Business Review.
Other titles: Harvard Business Review's 10 must reads 2021 | HBR's 10 must
    reads (Series)
Description: Boston, Massachusetts : Harvard Business Review Press, [2021]
    | Series: HBR's 10 must reads series | Includes index.
Identifiers: LCCN 2020012279 (print) | LCCN 2020012280 (ebook) | ISBN
    9781647820039 (paperback) | ISBN 9781647820046 (ebook)
Subjects: LCSH: Management.
Classification: LCC HD31.2 .H368 2021 (print) | LCC HD31.2 (ebook) | DDC
    658—dc23
LC record available at https://lccn.loc.gov/2020012279
LC ebook record available at https://lccn.loc.gov/2020012280

ISBN: 978-1-64782-003-9
eISBN: 978-1-64782-004-6

Contents

Editors' Note

Every year when our editorial group meets to assemble this collection, a few notable themes emerge. As we made our final selections, late last winter, the most prominent was the strange pace of change. Companies are adapting now to climate change—a threat that is both new and decades in the making, a danger to business and society that is already having direct consequences but whose ultimate effects have barely been felt. Similarly, the emergence of AI in business has been dizzying—but the changes it has wrought over the past half-decade may turn out to be minor compared with the tsunami of automation on the horizon. Inclusivity in the workplace has made great steps forward—companies are now considering how to provide a supportive environment for transgender people at work—even as the advancement of African-American leaders remains painfully slow. How are we to make sense of these swirling, contradictory changes? Is the practice of management improving faster than ever, or is it stuck in neutral?

A few weeks after we met, the coronavirus went worldwide. In what felt like an instant, all our notions about the pace of change and our predictions for the year 2021 were obliterated.

As of this writing, the world is many weeks into the first global pandemic lockdown. It's uncertain how much of this newly remote way of life is a passing moment and how much is the beginning of a new normal. Today parts of China, Europe, and the United States are beginning to ease restrictions, and we're looking ahead to the coming days with a mix of hope and fear.

Throughout, HBR's role has held steady. Our mission, "to improve the practice of management in a changing world," remains urgent. In recent weeks some forward-looking companies have shifted away from immediate crisis management and begun to reorganize for resilience and innovation in a time dominated by a desolate economic outlook, new habits, and employees who are hurting deeply. Effective management is needed more than ever to balance the existential imperatives of today with leadership for the long term.

Many pieces in this collection take on new meaning when seen through the lens of the pandemic. Cross-silo collaboration will be necessary not just to reinvent your own company but to lead the promising and innovative projects that will help the world rebound. Effective feedback and coaching become more challenging when workers are remote, lonely, and on the verge of burnout. Diversity and inclusion, along with fair hiring practices, are all the more pressing when so many jobs are at risk. The challenges faced by dual-career couples and working parents become clearer every time a video meeting is interrupted by a Zoom-bombing toddler.

Meanwhile, the other starkly urgent issue of our time—climate change—looms larger than ever. If the pandemic has one positive outcome, it's the growth of our capacity to imagine what a collective disaster looks like. The veneer of invincibility on industry and humanity has dissolved. Covid-19 has put the consequences of inaction in plain sight and demonstrated that preventable yet irreparable damage can occur in *days*. We hope that business will be inspired to take brave action now on climate.

This book, our final selection of articles from the prepandemic era, points to a world ready for great change yet stuck in old habits and paradigms. The best HBR articles are enduring; as you read through them, look for practices that will help your business survive the crisis and reach new heights tomorrow.

For years managers have been encouraged to give candid feedback on just about everything workers do. But, as Marcus Buckingham and Ashley Goodall argue in **"The Feedback Fallacy,"** that doesn't actually help employees thrive, because identifying failure and telling people how to correct it will never produce great performance. Instead, when managers see a great outcome, they should acknowledge the person who created it and share their impression of why it was a success. That fosters learning by showing what we're doing well. This was one of HBR's most popular—and widely debated—articles in many years.

Promising innovation and business opportunities require collaboration among functions, offices, and organizations. To realize them, companies must get people working together across boundaries, but that's a challenge for many leaders. **"Cross-Silo Leadership,"** by Tiziana Casciaro, Amy C. Edmondson, and Sujin Jang, explores the activities leaders can support to promote horizontal teamwork in their companies and help employees connect with and learn from people who think very differently from them.

At most large U.S. and multinational enterprises, diversity and inclusion have become imperatives, but the progress of African Americans remains slow. In **"Toward a Racially Just Workplace,"** Laura Morgan Roberts and Anthony J. Mayo argue that companies can take specific steps to achieve racial fairness. They can shift their focus from the most lucrative thing to the right thing, encourage open conversations about race, revamp diversity and inclusion programs to clarify goals and focus on proactive steps, and manage development across all career stages.

Thanks to technologies that enable constant, customized interactions, companies are building deeper ties with their customers. They can now address customer needs the moment they arise—sometimes even earlier—and dramatically improve their customers' experiences, boost their own operational efficiencies, and gain competitive advantage. In **"The Age of Continuous Connection,"** Nicolaj Siggelkow and Christian Terwiesch identify four effective and connected strategies: filling customers' requests quickly and seamlessly; presenting individually tailored recommendations; reminding people of their needs and goals and nudging them to act; and anticipating what people want and delivering it without even being asked.

Innovative cultures are generally depicted as fun, characterized by a tolerance for failure and a willingness to experiment, and seen as psychologically safe, highly collaborative, and nonhierarchical. And research suggests that those qualities translate into better innovative performance. Even so, they're hard to create and sustain. Gary P. Pisano explains why in the McKinsey Award–winning **"The Hard Truth about Innovative Cultures."** Easy-to-like behaviors must be counterbalanced by some tougher ones: intolerance for incompetence, rigorous discipline, brutal candor, a high level of individual accountability, and strong leadership. Unless the tensions created by this paradox are carefully managed, attempts to create an innovative culture will fail.

Despite growing public awareness of the struggles that transgender individuals often face, many employers remain ill-equipped to create supportive policies and workplace cultures. Christian N. Thoroughgood, Katina B. Sawyer, and Jennica R. Webster, the authors of **"Creating a Trans-Inclusive Workplace,"** demonstrate how companies can more effectively attract, retain, and promote the health and success of these workers through four areas of intervention: basic signs of trans inclusivity involving bathroom use, dress codes, and pronouns; effective support for gender transitions; trans-specific diversity trainings; and interventions to build resiliency.

Many executives assume that customer data can give you an unbeatable edge. The more customers you have, the more data you can gather, and analyzing that data allows you to offer a better product that attracts more customers. Although this thinking is usually wrong, Andrei Hagiu and Julian Wright show in **"When Data Creates Competitive Advantage"** that under the right conditions, customer data can help build competitive defenses. It all depends on whether the data offers high and lasting value, is proprietary, leads to improvements that can't be easily imitated, or generates insights that can be quickly incorporated. Only then will the virtuous cycle of data-enabled learning take off.

Companies now outsource much of the hiring process to vendors that in turn use subcontractors to scour LinkedIn and social media for potential candidates. When applications come in, software sifts through them for key words that hiring managers want to see. According to Peter Cappelli in **"Your Approach to Hiring Is All Wrong,"** vendors offer an array of smart-sounding tools that claim to predict who will be a good hire—but it's yet to be proved that they produce satisfactory results. This article explores what's wrong with today's recruiting and hiring—failing to post jobs internally, advertising jobs that don't exist, misunderstanding the strengths and weaknesses of machine-learning models—and how to fix it.

In her research Jennifer Petriglieri, the author of **"How Dual-Career Couples Make It Work,"** found that such couples tend to experience three transitions when they are particularly vulnerable: when they first learn to work together as a couple; when they go through a midcareer or a midlife reinvention; and as they reach the final stages of their careers. Those who communicate during each transition about deeper work and personal issues such as values, boundaries, and fears have a better chance of emerging stronger from it, fulfilled both in their relationships and in their careers.

The use of artificial intelligence in business is no longer novel, yet most companies have run only ad hoc projects or applied AI in just a single business process. The key to capturing the full AI opportunity, according to Tim Fountaine, Brian McCarthy, and Tamim Saleh in **"Building the AI-Powered Organization,"** is to understand the organizational and cultural barriers faced by AI initiatives and work to lower them. That means shifting workers away from traditional mindsets—such as relying on top-down decision making—which often run counter to what's needed for AI. Leaders can also set up AI projects for success by conveying their urgency and benefits; investing heavily in AI education and adoption; and accounting for the company's AI maturity, business complexity, and innovation pace when deciding how work should be organized.

It's well past time to recognize that aggressive climate action is necessary if humanity is to survive and thrive. What's more, climate change is damaging the economy and company bottom lines *today*, not in some distant future. And although many large companies are cutting carbon emissions, their efforts are sadly inadequate given the scale of the crisis. In **"Leading a New Era of Climate Action,"** Andrew Winston recommends three approaches: using political influence to demand aggressive climate policies; empowering suppliers, customers, and employees to drive change; and rethinking investments and business models to eliminate waste and carbon. Companies must mobilize now to address this global threat.

Our final article is a special addition from HBR.org. On one of our first days of obligatory remote work during the coronavirus pandemic, a few dozen of us found ourselves at home, looking at one another in a not-yet-commonplace grid of small, familiar faces. As in so many meetings in the early days of the crisis, we were talking about how we felt, and one colleague mentioned that she was experiencing grief. Heads nodded in all the panes. Editor Scott Berinato was inspired to reach out to David Kessler, a coauthor of *On Grief and Grieving: Finding the Meaning of Grief through the Five Stages of Loss.* Within a few days the interview **"That Discomfort You're Feeling Is Grief"** had reached an enormous worldwide audience and become the most-read article in the history of hbr.org. Kessler and Berinato discuss the stages of grief, techniques to make the feeling less intense, and the importance of a sixth stage—*meaning*—which can help us fathom painful events and become stronger as a result.

Finding the right words to open this book during the time of Covid-19 was a challenge. Books take a while to be published—so what is the right way to talk about an issue that's changing daily in a note that won't be read for months? Yet it gives us hope to know that you're still here with us and looking for ideas and inspiration from the best of HBR. We wish you, your family, and your teams good health during this surreal and scary time, and hope that our annual collection will help you and your business carve a bold path forward this year.

—The Editors

**HBR'S
10
MUST
READS**

The definitive
management ideas
of the year from
Harvard Business Review.

2021

The Feedback Fallacy

by Marcus Buckingham and Ashley Goodall

THE DEBATE ABOUT FEEDBACK AT WORK ISN'T NEW. Since at least the middle of the last century, the question of how to get employees to improve has generated a good deal of opinion and research. But recently the discussion has taken on new intensity.

The ongoing experiment in "radical transparency" at Bridgewater Associates and the culture at Netflix, which the *Wall Street Journal* recently described as "encouraging harsh feedback" and subjecting workers to "intense and awkward" real-time 360s, are but two examples of the overriding belief that the way to increase performance in companies is through rigorous, frequent, candid, pervasive, and often critical feedback.

How should we give and receive feedback? we wonder. How much, and how often, and using which new app? And, given the hoopla over the approaches of Bridgewater and Netflix, how hard-edged and fearlessly candid should we be? Behind those questions, however, is another question that we're missing, and it's a crucial one. The search for ways to give and receive better feedback assumes that feedback is always useful. But the only reason we're pursuing it is to help people do better. And when we examine *that*—asking, *How can we help each person thrive and excel?*—we find that the answers take us in a different direction.

To be clear, instruction—telling people what steps to follow or what factual knowledge they're lacking—can be truly useful: That's why we have checklists in airplane cockpits and, more recently, in operating rooms. There is indeed a right way for a nurse to give an injection safely, and if you as a novice nurse miss one of the steps, or if you're unaware of critical facts about a patient's condition, then someone should tell you. But the occasions when the actions or knowledge necessary to minimally perform a job can be objectively defined in advance are rare and becoming rarer. What we mean by "feedback" is very different. Feedback is about telling people what we think of their performance and how they should do it better—whether they're giving an effective presentation, leading a team, or creating a strategy. And on that, the research is clear: Telling people what we think of their performance doesn't help them thrive and excel, and telling people how we think they should improve actually *hinders* learning.

Underpinning the current conviction that feedback is an unalloyed good are three theories that we in the business world commonly accept as truths. The first is that other people are more aware than you are of your weaknesses, and that the best way to help you, therefore, is for them to show you what you cannot see for yourself. We can call this our *theory of the source of truth.* You do not realize that your suit is shabby, that your presentation is boring, or that your voice is grating, so it is up to your colleagues to tell you as plainly as possible "where you stand." If they didn't, you would never know, and this would be bad.

The second belief is that the process of learning is like filling up an empty vessel: You lack certain abilities you need to acquire, so your colleagues should teach them to you. We can call this our *theory of learning.* If you're in sales, how can you possibly close deals if you don't learn the competency of "mirroring and matching" the prospect? If you're a teacher, how can you improve if you don't learn and practice the steps in the latest team-teaching technique or "flipped classroom" format? The thought is that you can't—and that you need feedback to develop the skills you're missing.

And the third belief is that great performance is universal, analyzable, and describable, and that once defined, it can be transferred from one person to another, regardless of who each individual is. Hence you can, with feedback about what excellence looks like,

Idea in Brief

The Challenge

Managers today are bombarded with calls to give feedback—constantly, directly, and critically. But it turns out that telling people what we think of their performance and how they can do better is not the best way to help them excel and, in fact, can hinder development.

The Reality

Research shows that, first, we aren't the reliable raters of other people's performance that we think we are; second, criticism inhibits the brain's ability to learn; and, third, excellence is idiosyncratic, can't be defined in advance, and isn't the opposite of failure. Managers can't "correct" a person's way to excellence.

The Solution

Managers need to help their team members see what's working, stopping them with a "Yes! That!" and sharing their experience of what the person did well.

understand where you fall short of this ideal and then strive to remedy your shortcomings. We can call this our *theory of excellence.* If you're a manager, your boss might show you the company's supervisor-behaviors model, hold you up against it, and tell you what you need to do to more closely hew to it. If you aspire to lead, your firm might use a 360-degree feedback tool to measure you against its predefined leadership competencies and then suggest various courses or experiences that will enable you to acquire the competencies that your results indicate you lack.

What these three theories have in common is self-centeredness: They take our own expertise and what we are sure is our colleagues' inexpertise as givens; they assume that my way is necessarily your way. But as it turns out, in extrapolating from what creates our own performance to what might create performance in others, we overreach.

Research reveals that none of these theories is true. The more we depend on them, and the more technology we base on them, the *less* learning and productivity we will get from others. To understand why and to see the path to a more effective way of improving performance, let's look more closely at each theory in turn.

The Source of Truth

The first problem with feedback is that humans are unreliable raters of other humans. Over the past 40 years psychometricians have shown in study after study that people don't have the objectivity to hold in their heads a stable definition of an abstract quality, such as *business acumen* or *assertiveness*, and then accurately evaluate someone else on it. Our evaluations are deeply colored by our own understanding of what we're rating others on, our own sense of what good looks like for a particular competency, our harshness or leniency as raters, and our own inherent and unconscious biases. This phenomenon is called the *idiosyncratic rater effect*, and it's large (more than half of your rating of someone else reflects your characteristics, not hers) and resilient (no training can lessen it). In other words, the research shows that feedback is more distortion than truth.

This is why, despite all the training available on how to *receive* feedback, it's such hard work: Recipients have to struggle through this forest of distortion in search of something that they recognize as themselves.

And because your feedback to others is always more you than them, it leads to systematic error, which is magnified when ratings are considered in aggregate. There are only two sorts of measurement error in the world: *random* error, which you can reduce by averaging many readings; and *systematic* error, which you can't. Unfortunately, we all seem to have left math class remembering the former and not the latter. We've built all our performance and leadership feedback tools as though assessment errors are random, and they're not. They're systematic.

Consider color blindness. If we ask a color-blind person to rate the redness of a particular rose, we won't trust his feedback—we know that he is incapable of seeing, let alone "rating," red. His error isn't random; it's predictable and explainable, and it stems from a flaw in his measurement system; hence, it's systematic. If we then decide to ask seven more color-blind people to rate the redness of our rose, their errors will be equally systematic, and averaging their ratings won't get us any closer to determining the actual redness of the rose.

In fact, it's worse than this. Adding up all the inaccurate redness ratings—"gray," "pretty gray," "whitish gray," "muddy brown," and so on—and averaging them leads us *further away* both from learning anything reliable about the individuals' personal experiences of the rose and from the actual truth of how red our rose really is.

What the research has revealed is that we're all color-blind when it comes to abstract attributes, such as *strategic thinking, potential,* and *political savvy.* Our inability to rate others on them is predictable and explainable—it is systematic. We cannot remove the error by adding more data inputs and averaging them out, and doing that actually makes the error bigger.

Worse still, although science has long since proven that we are color-blind, in the business world we assume we're clear-eyed. Deep down we don't think we make very many errors at all. We think we're reliable raters of others. We think we're a source of truth. We aren't. We're a source of error.

When a feedback instrument surveys eight colleagues about your business acumen, your score of 3.79 is far greater a distortion than if it simply surveyed one person about you—the 3.79 number is *all* noise, no signal. Given that (a) we're starting to see more of this sort of data-based feedback, (b) this data on you will likely be kept by your company for a very long time, and (c) it will be used to pay, promote, train, and deploy or fire you, you should be worried about just how fundamentally flawed it really is.

The only realm in which humans are an unimpeachable source of truth is that of their own feelings and experiences. Doctors have long known this. When they check up on you post-op, they'll ask, "On a scale of one to 10, with 10 being high, how would you rate your pain?" And if you say, "Five," the doctor may then prescribe all manner of treatments, but what she's unlikely to do is challenge you on your "five." It doesn't make sense, no matter how many operations she has done, to tell you your "five" is wrong, and that, actually, this morning your pain is a "three." It doesn't make sense to try to parse what you mean by "five," and whether any cultural differences might indicate that your "five" is not, in fact, a real "five." It doesn't make sense to hold calibration sessions with other doctors to ensure

5

that your "five" is the same as the other "fives" in the rooms down the hall. Instead, she can be confident that you are the best judge of your pain and that all she can know for sure is that you will be feeling better when you rate your pain lower. Your rating is yours, not hers.

Just as your doctor doesn't know the truth of your pain, we don't know the truth about our colleagues, at least not in any objective way. You may read that workers today—especially Millennials—want to know where they stand. You may occasionally have team members ask you to tell them where they stand, objectively. You may feel that it's your duty to try to answer these questions. But you can't—none of us can. All we can do—and it's not nothing—is share our own feelings and experiences, our own reactions. Thus we can tell someone whether his voice grates *on us*; whether he's persuasive *to us*; whether his presentation is boring *to us*. We may not be able to tell him where he stands, but we can tell him where he stands *with us*. Those are our truths, not his. This is a humbler claim, but at least it's accurate.

How We Learn

Another of our collective theories is that feedback contains useful information, and that this information is the magic ingredient that will accelerate someone's learning. Again, the research points in the opposite direction. Learning is less a function of adding something that isn't there than it is of recognizing, reinforcing, and refining what already is. There are two reasons for this.

The first is that, neurologically, we grow more in our areas of greater ability (our strengths are our development areas). The brain continues to develop throughout life, but each person's does so differently. Because of your genetic inheritance and the oddities of your early childhood environment, your brain's wiring is utterly unique. Some parts of it have tight thickets of synaptic connections, while others are far less dense, and these patterns are different from one person to the next. According to brain science, people grow far more neurons and synaptic connections where they already have the most neurons and synaptic connections. In other words, each brain grows most where it's already strongest. As Joseph LeDoux, a professor of neuroscience at New York University, memorably described it, "Added connections are therefore more like new buds on a branch rather than new branches." Through this lens, learning looks a lot like building, little by little, on the unique patterns already there within you. Which in turn means learning has to start by finding and understanding those patterns—your patterns, not someone else's.

Second, getting attention to our strengths from others catalyzes learning, whereas attention to our weaknesses smothers it. Neurological science also shows what happens to us when other people focus on what's working within us instead of remediating what isn't. In one experiment scientists split students into two groups. To one group they gave positive coaching, asking the students about their dreams and how they'd go about achieving them. The scientists probed the other group about homework and what the students thought they were doing wrong and needed to fix. While those conversations were happening, the scientists hooked each student up to a functional magnetic resonance imaging machine to see which parts of the brain were most activated in response to these different sorts of attention.

In the brains of the students asked about what they needed to correct, the sympathetic nervous system lit up. This is the "fight or flight" system, which mutes the other parts of the brain and allows us to focus only on the information most necessary to survive. Your brain responds to critical feedback as a threat and narrows its activity. The strong negative emotion produced by criticism "inhibits access to existing neural circuits and invokes cognitive, emotional, and perceptual impairment," psychology and business professor Richard Boyatzis said in summarizing the researchers' findings.

Focusing people on their shortcomings or gaps doesn't enable learning. It impairs it.

In the students who focused on their dreams and how they might achieve them, the sympathetic nervous system was not activated. What lit up instead was the parasympathetic nervous system, sometimes referred to as the "rest and digest" system. To quote Boyatzis again: "The parasympathetic nervous system . . . stimulates adult neurogenesis (i.e., growth of new neurons) . . . , a sense of well-being, better immune system functioning, and cognitive, emotional, and perceptual openness."

What findings such as these show us is, first, that learning happens when we see how we might do something better by adding some new nuance or expansion to our own understanding. Learning rests on our grasp of what we're doing well, not on what we're doing poorly, and certainly not on someone else's sense of what we're doing poorly. And second, that we learn most when someone else pays attention to what's working within us and asks us to cultivate it intelligently. We're often told that the key to learning is to get out of our comfort zones, but these findings contradict that particular chestnut: Take us very far out of our comfort zones, and our brains stop paying attention to anything other than surviving the experience. It's clear that we learn most in our comfort zones, because that's where our neural pathways are most concentrated. It's where we're most open to possibility, most creative, insightful, and productive. That's where feedback must meet us—in our moments of flow.

Excellence

We spend the bulk of our working lives pursuing excellence in the belief that while defining it is easy, the really hard part is codifying how we and everyone else on our team should get there. We've got it backward: Excellence in any endeavor is almost impossible to define, and yet getting there, for each of us, is relatively easy.

Excellence is idiosyncratic. Take funniness—the ability to make others laugh. If you watch early Steve Martin clips, you might land on the idea that excellence at it means strumming a banjo, waggling your knees, and wailing, "I'm a wild and crazy guy!" But watch Jerry Seinfeld, and you might conclude that it means talking about nothing in a slightly annoyed, exasperated tone. And if you watch Sarah Silverman, you might think to yourself, no, it's being caustic, blunt, and rude in an incongruously affectless way. At this point you may begin to perceive the truth that "funny" is inherent to the person.

Watch an NBA game, and you may think to yourself, "Yes, most of them are tall and athletic, but boy, not only does each player have a different role on the team, but even the players in the same role on the same team seem to do it differently." Examine something as specific and as limited as the free throws awarded after fouls, and you'll learn that not only do the top two free-throw shooters in history have utterly different styles, but one of them, Rick Barry—the best ever on the day he retired (look him up)—didn't even throw overhand.

Excellence seems to be inextricably and wonderfully intertwined with whoever demonstrates it. Each person's version of it is uniquely shaped and is an expression of that person's individuality. Which means that, for each of us, excellence is easy, in that it is a natural, fluid, and intelligent expression of our best extremes. It can be cultivated, but it's unforced.

Excellence is also not the opposite of failure. But in virtually all aspects of human endeavor, people assume that it is and that if they study what leads to pathological functioning and do the reverse—or replace what they found missing—they can create optimal functioning. That assumption is flawed. Study disease and you will learn a lot about disease and precious little about health. Eradicating depression will get you no closer to joy. Divorce is mute on the topic of happy marriage. Exit interviews with employees who leave tell you nothing about why others stay. If you study failure, you'll learn a lot about failure but nothing about how to achieve excellence. Excellence has its own pattern.

And it's even more problematic than that. Excellence and failure often have a lot in common. So if you study ineffective leaders and observe that they have big egos, and then argue that good leaders should not have big egos, you will lead people astray. Why? Because when you do personality assessments with highly effective leaders, you discover that they have very strong egos as well. Telling someone that you must lose your ego to be a good leader is flawed advice. Likewise, if you study poor salespeople, discover that they take rejection personally, and then tell a budding salesperson to avoid doing the same, your advice will be misguided. Why? Because rigorous studies of the best salespeople reveal that they take rejection deeply personally, too.

As it happens, you find that effective leaders put their egos in the service of others, not themselves, and that effective salespeople take rejection personally because they are personally invested in the sale—but the point is that you will never find these things out by studying *ineffective* performance.

Since excellence is idiosyncratic and cannot be learned by studying failure, we can never help another person succeed by holding her performance up against a prefabricated model of excellence, giving her feedback on where she misses the model, and telling her to plug the gaps. That approach will only ever get her to adequate performance. Point out the grammatical flaws in an essay, ask the writer to fix the flaws, and while you may get an essay with good grammar, you won't get a piece of writing that transports the reader. Show a new teacher when her students lost interest and tell her what to do to fix this, and while you may now have a teacher whose students don't fall asleep in class, you won't have one whose students necessarily learn any more.

How to Help People Excel

If we continue to spend our time identifying failure as we see it and giving people feedback about how to avoid it, we'll languish in the business of adequacy. To get into the excellence business we need some new techniques:

Look for outcomes

Excellence is an outcome, so take note of when a prospect leans into a sales pitch, a project runs smoothly, or an angry customer suddenly calms down. Then turn to the team member who created the outcome and say, "That! Yes, that!" By doing this, you'll stop the flow of work for a moment and pull your colleague's attention back toward something she just did that really worked.

There's a story about how legendary Dallas Cowboys coach Tom Landry turned around his struggling team. While the other teams were reviewing missed tackles and dropped balls, Landry instead

The Right Way to Help Colleagues Excel

IF YOU WANT to get into the excellence business, here are some examples of language to try.

Instead of	Try
Can I give you some feedback?	Here's my reaction.
Good job!	Here are three things that really worked for me. What was going through your mind when you did them?
Here's what you should do.	Here's what I would do.
Here's where you need to improve.	Here's what worked best for me, and here's why.
That didn't really work.	When you did x, I felt y or I didn't get that.
You need to improve your communication skills.	Here's exactly where you started to lose me.
You need to be more responsive.	When I don't hear from you, I worry that we're not on the same page.
You lack strategic thinking.	I'm struggling to understand your plan.
You should do x [in response to a request for advice].	What do you feel you're struggling with, and what have you done in the past that's worked in a similar situation?

combed through footage of previous games and created for each player a highlight reel of when he had done something easily, naturally, and effectively. Landry reasoned that while the number of wrong ways to do something was infinite, the number of right ways, for any particular player, was not. It was knowable, and the best way to discover it was to look at plays where that person had done it excellently. From now on, he told each team member, "we only replay your winning plays."

Now on one level he was doing this to make his team members feel better about themselves because he knew the power of praise. But according to the story, Landry wasn't nearly as interested in praise as he was in learning. His instincts told him that each person would improve his performance most if he could see, in slow motion, what his own personal version of excellence looked like.

You can do the same. Whenever you see one of your people do something that worked for you, that rocked your world just a little, stop for a minute and highlight it. By helping your team member recognize what excellence looks like for her—by saying, "That! Yes, that!"—you're offering her the chance to gain an insight; you're highlighting a pattern that is already there within her so that she can recognize it, anchor it, re-create it, and refine it. That is learning.

Replay your instinctive reactions
Unlike Landry, you're not going to be able to videotape your people. Instead, learn how to replay to them your own personal reactions. The key is not to tell someone how well she's performed or how good she is. While simple praise isn't a bad thing, you are by no means the authority on what objectively good performance is, and instinctively she knows this. Instead, describe what you experienced when her moment of excellence caught your attention. There's nothing more believable and more authoritative than sharing what you saw from her and how it made you feel. Use phrases such as "This is how that came across for me," or "This is what that made me think," or even just "Did you see what you did there?" Those are your reactions— they are your truth—and when you relay them in specific detail, you aren't judging or rating or fixing her; you're simply reflecting to her the unique "dent" she just made in the world, as seen through your eyes. And precisely because it isn't a judgment or a rating, it is at once more humble and more powerful.

On the flip side, if you're the team member, whenever your team leader catches you doing something right, ask her to pause and describe her reaction to you. If she says, "Good job!" ask, "Which bit? What did you see that seemed to work well?" Again, the point of this isn't to pile on the praise. The point is to explore the nature of excellence, and this is surely a better object for all the energy currently being pointed at "radical transparency" and the like. We're so close to our own performance that it's hard to get perspective on it and see its patterns and components. Ask for your leader's help in rendering the unconscious, conscious—so that you can understand it, improve at it, and, most important, do it again.

Never lose sight of your highest-priority interrupt

In computing, a high-priority interrupt happens when something requires a computer processor's immediate attention, and the machine halts normal operations and jumps the urgent issue to the head of the processing queue. Like computer processors, team leaders have quite a few things that demand their attention and force them to act. Many of them are problems. If you see something go off the rails—a poorly handled call, a missed meeting, a project gone awry—the instinct will kick in to stop everything to tell someone what she did wrong and what she needs to do to fix it. This instinct is by no means misguided: If your team member screws something up, you have to deal with it. But remember that when you do, you're merely remediating—and that remediating not only inhibits learning but also gets you no closer to excellent performance. As we've seen, conjuring excellence from your team members requires a different focus from you. If you see somebody doing something that really works, stopping her and dissecting it with her isn't only a high-priority interrupt, it is your *highest*-priority interrupt. As you replay each small moment of excellence to your team member, you'll ease her into the "rest and digest" state of mind. Her understanding of what excellence looks and feels like within her will become more vivid, her brain will become more receptive to new information and will make connections to other inputs found in other regions of her brain, and she will learn and grow and get better.

Explore the present, past, and future

When people come to you asking for feedback on their performance or what they might need to fix to get promoted, try this:

Start with the *present*. If a team member approaches you with a problem, he's dealing with it *now*. He's feeling weak or challenged, and you have to address that. But rather than tackling the problem head-on, ask your colleague to tell you three things that are working for him *right now*. These things might be related to the situation or entirely separate. They might be significant or trivial. Just ask the question, and you're priming him with oxytocin—which is sometimes called the "love drug" but which here is better thought of as the "creativity drug." Getting him to think about specific things that are going well will alter his brain chemistry so that he can be open to new solutions and new ways of thinking or acting.

Next, go to the *past*. Ask him, "When you had a problem like this in the past, what did you do that worked?" Much of our life happens in patterns, so it's highly likely that he has encountered this problem at least a few times before. On one of those occasions he will almost certainly have found some way forward, some action or insight or connection that enabled him to move out of the mess. Get him thinking about that and seeing it in his mind's eye: what he actually felt and did, and what happened next.

Finally, turn to the *future*. Ask your team member, "What do you already know you need to do? What do you already know works in this situation?" By all means offer up one or two of your own experiences to see if they might clarify his own. But operate under the assumption that he already knows the solution—you're just helping him recognize it.

The emphasis here should not be on whys—"Why didn't that work?" "Why do you think you should do that?"—because those lead both of you into a fuzzy world of conjecture and concepts. Instead, focus on the whats—"What do you actually want to have happen?" "What are a couple of actions you could take right now?" These sorts of questions yield concrete answers, in which your colleague can find his actual self doing actual things in the near-term future.

How to give people feedback is one of the hottest topics in business today. The arguments for radical candor and unvarnished and pervasive transparency have a swagger to them, almost as if to imply that only the finest and bravest of us can face these truths with nerveless self-assurance, that those of us who recoil at the thought of working in a climate of continual judgment are condemned to mediocrity, and that as leaders our ability to look our colleagues squarely in the eye and lay out their faults without blinking is a measure of our integrity.

But at best, this fetish with feedback is good only for correcting mistakes—in the rare cases where the right steps are known and can be evaluated objectively. And at worst, it's toxic, because what we want from our people—and from ourselves—is not, for the most part, tidy adherence to a procedure agreed upon in advance or, for that matter, the ability to expose one another's flaws. It's that people contribute their own unique and growing talents to a common good, when that good is ever-evolving, when we are, for all the right reasons, making it up as we go along. Feedback has nothing to offer to that.

We humans do not do well when someone whose intentions are unclear tells us where we stand, how good we "really" are, and what we must do to fix ourselves. We excel *only* when people who know us and care about us tell us what they experience and what they feel, and in particular when they see something within us that really works.

Originally published in March–April 2019. Reprint R1902G

Cross-Silo Leadership

by Tiziana Casciaro, Amy C. Edmondson, and Sujin Jang

THOUGH MOST EXECUTIVES recognize the importance of breaking down silos to help people collaborate across boundaries, they struggle to make it happen. That's understandable: It is devilishly difficult.

Think about your own relationships at work—the people you report to and those who report to you, for starters. Now consider the people in other functions, units, or geographies whose work touches yours in some way. Which relationships get prioritized in your day-to-day job?

We've posed that question to managers, engineers, salespeople, and consultants in companies around the world. The response we get is almost always the same: vertical relationships.

But when we ask, "Which relationships are most important for creating value for customers?" the answers flip. Today the vast majority of innovation and business-development opportunities lie in the interfaces between functions, offices, or organizations. In short, the integrated solutions that most customers want—but companies wrestle with developing—require horizontal collaboration.

The value of horizontal teamwork is widely recognized. Employees who can reach outside their silos to find colleagues with complementary expertise learn more, sell more, and gain skills faster. Harvard's Heidi Gardner has found that firms with more cross-boundary collaboration achieve greater customer loyalty and higher margins. As innovation hinges more and more on interdisciplinary cooperation, digitalization transforms business at a breakneck pace, and globalization increasingly requires people to work across national borders, the demand for executives who can lead projects at interfaces keeps rising.

Our research and consulting work with hundreds of executives and managers in dozens of organizations confirms both the need for and the challenge of horizontal collaboration. "There's no doubt. We should focus on big projects that call for integration across practices," a partner in a global accounting firm told us. "That's where our greatest distinctive value is developed. But most of us confine ourselves to the smaller projects that we can handle within our practice areas. It's frustrating." A senior partner in a leading consulting firm put it slightly differently: "You know you should swim farther to catch a bigger fish, but it is a lot easier to swim in your own pond and catch a bunch of small fish."

One way to break down silos is to redesign the formal organizational structure. But that approach has limits: It's costly, confusing, and slow. Worse, every new structure solves some problems but creates others. That's why we've focused on identifying activities that facilitate boundary crossing. We've found that people can be trained to see and connect with pools of expertise throughout their organizations and to work better with colleagues who think very differently from them. The core challenges of operating effectively at interfaces are simple: *learning* about people on the other side and *relating* to them. But simple does not mean easy; human beings have always struggled to understand and relate to those who are different.

Leaders need to help people develop the capacity to overcome these challenges on both individual and organizational levels. That means providing training in and support for four practices that enable effective interface work.

1. Develop and Deploy Cultural Brokers

Fortunately, in most companies there are people who already excel at interface collaboration. They usually have experiences and relationships that span multiple sectors, functions, or domains

Idea in Brief

The Challenge

Innovation initiatives, globalization, and digitalization increasingly require people to collaborate across functional and national boundaries. But breaking down silos remains frustratingly difficult.

The Cause

Employees don't know how to identify expertise outside their own work domains and struggle to understand the perspectives of colleagues who think very differently from them.

The Solution

Leaders can help employees connect with and relate to people across organizational divides by doing four things: developing and deploying "cultural brokers," who help groups overcome differences; encouraging and training workers to ask the right questions; getting people to see things through others' eyes; and broadening everyone's vision of networks of expertise inside and outside the company.

and informally serve as links between them. We call these people *cultural brokers.* In studies involving more than 2,000 global teams, one of us—Sujin—found that diverse teams containing a cultural broker significantly outperformed diverse teams without one. (See "The Most Creative Teams Have a Specific Type of Cultural Diversity," hbr.org, July 24, 2018.) Companies should identify these individuals and help them increase their impact.

Cultural brokers promote cross-boundary work in one of two ways: by acting as a *bridge* or as an *adhesive.*

A bridge offers himself as a go-between, allowing people in different functions or geographies to collaborate with minimal disruption to their day-to-day routine. Bridges are most effective when they have considerable knowledge of both sides and can figure out what each one needs. This is why the champagne and spirits distributor Moët Hennessy España hired two enologists, or wine experts, to help coordinate the work of its marketing and sales groups, which had a history of miscommunication and conflict. The enologists could relate to both groups equally: They could speak to marketers about the emotional content (the ephemeral "bouquet") of brands, while also providing pragmatic salespeople with details on the distinctive features of products they needed to win over retailers. Understanding both worlds, the enologists were able to communicate the rationale for each group's modus operandi to the other, allowing marketing and sales to work more synergistically even without directly interacting. This kind of cultural brokerage is efficient because it lets disparate parties work around differences without investing in learning the other side's perspective or changing how they work. It's especially valuable for one-off collaborations or when the company is under intense time pressure to deliver results.

Adhesives, in contrast, bring people together and help build mutual understanding and lasting relationships. Take one manager we spoke with at National Instruments, a global producer of automated test equipment. He frequently connects colleagues from different regions and functions. "I think of it as building up the relationships between them," he told us. "If a colleague needs to work with someone in another office or function, I would tell them, 'OK, here's the person to call.' Then I'd take the time to sit down and say, 'Well, let me tell you a little bit about how these guys work.'" Adhesives facilitate collaboration by vouching for people and helping them decipher one another's language. Unlike bridges, adhesives develop others' capacity to work across a boundary in the future without their assistance.

Company leaders can build both bridging and adhesive capabilities in their organizations by hiring people with multifunctional or multicultural backgrounds who have the strong interpersonal skills needed to build rapport with multiple parties. Because it takes resilience to work with people across cultural divides, firms should also look for a *growth mindset*—the desire to learn and to take on challenges and "stretch" opportunities.

In addition, leaders can develop more brokers by giving people at all levels the chance to move into roles that expose them to multiple parts of the company. This, by the way, is good training for general managers and is what many rotational leadership-development programs aim to accomplish. Claudine Wolfe, the head of talent and development at the global insurer Chubb, maintains that the company's capacity to serve customers around the world rests on giving top performers opportunities to work in different geographies and cultivate an international mindset. "We give people their critical development experiences steeped in the job, in the region," she says. "They get coaching in the cultural norms and the language, but then they live it and internalize it. They go to the local bodega, take notice of the products on the shelves, have conversations with the merchant, and learn what it really means to live in that environment."

Matrix organizational structures, in which people report to two (or more) groups, can also help develop cultural brokers. Despite their inherent challenges (they can be infuriatingly hard to navigate without strong leadership and accountability), matrices get people used to operating at interfaces.

We're not saying that everyone in your organization needs to be a full-fledged cultural broker. But consciously expanding the ranks of brokers and deploying them to grease the wheels of collaboration can go a long way.

2. Encourage People to Ask the Right Questions

It's nearly impossible to work across boundaries without asking a lot of questions. Inquiry is critical because what we see and take for granted on one side of an interface is not the same as what people experience on the other side.

Indeed, a study of more than 1,000 middle managers at a large bank that Tiziana conducted with Bill McEvily and Evelyn Zhang of the University of Toronto and Francesca Gino of Harvard Business School highlights the value of inquisitiveness in boundary-crossing work. It showed that managers with high levels of curiosity were more likely to build networks that spanned disconnected parts of the company.

But all of us are vulnerable to forgetting the crucial practice of asking questions as we move up the ladder. High-achieving people in particular frequently fail to wonder what others are seeing. Worse, when we do recognize that we don't know something, we may avoid asking a question out of (misguided) fear that it will make us look incompetent or weak. "Not asking questions is a big mistake many professionals make," Norma Kraay, the managing partner of talent for Deloitte Canada, told us. "Expert advisers want to offer a solution. That's what they're trained to do."

Leaders can encourage inquiry in two important ways—and in the process help create an organization where it's psychologically safe to ask questions.

Be a role model
When leaders show interest in what others are seeing and thinking by asking questions, it has a stunning effect: It prompts people in their organizations to do the same.

Asking questions also conveys the humility that more and more business leaders and researchers are pointing to as vital to success. According to Laszlo Bock, Google's former senior vice president of people operations, humble people are better at bringing others together to solve tough problems. In a fast-changing business environment, humility—not to be confused with false modesty—is simply a strength. Its power comes from realism (as in *It really is a complex, challenging world out there; if we don't work together, we don't stand a chance*).

Gino says one way a leader can make employees feel comfortable asking questions is by openly acknowledging when he or she doesn't know the answer. Another, she says, is by having days in which employees are explicitly encouraged to ask "Why?" "What if . . . ?" and "How might we . . . ?" (See "The Business Case for Curiosity," HBR, September–October 2018.)

Teach employees the art of inquiry
Training can help expand the range and frequency of questions employees ask and, according to Hal Gregersen of the MIT Leadership Center, can reinvigorate their sense of curiosity. But some questions are better than others. (See the exhibit "How to ask good questions.") And if you simply tell people to raise more questions, you might unleash interrogation tactics that inhibit rather than encourage the development of new perspectives. As MIT's Edgar

How to ask good questions

Common pitfalls	Effective inquiry
Start with yes-or-no questions.	Start with open-ended questions that minimize preconceptions. ("How are things going on your end?" "What does your group see as the key opportunity in this space?")
Continue asking overly general questions ("What's on your mind?") that may invite long off-point responses.	As collaborations develop, ask questions that focus on specific issues but allow people plenty of room to elaborate. ("What do you know about *x*?" "Can you explain how that works?")
Assume that you've grasped what speakers intended.	Check your understanding by summarizing what you're hearing and asking explicitly for corrections or missing elements. ("Does that sound right—am I missing anything?" "Can you help me fill in the gaps?")
Assume the collaboration process will take care of itself.	Periodically take time to inquire into others' experiences of the process or relationship. ("How do you think the project is going?" "What could we do to work together more effectively?")

Schein explains in his book *Humble Inquiry,* questions are the secret to productive work relationships—but they must be driven by genuine interest in understanding another's view.

It's also important to learn how to request information in the least biased way possible. This means asking open-ended questions that minimize preconceptions, rather than yes-or-no questions. For instance, "What do you see as the key opportunity in this space?" will generate a richer dialogue than "Do you think this is the right opportunity to pursue?"

As collaborations move forward, it's helpful for team leaders or project managers to raise queries that encourage others to dive more deeply into specific issues and express related ideas or experiences. "What do you know about *x*?" and "Can you explain how that works?" are two examples. These questions are focused but neither limit responses nor invite long discourses that stray too far from the issue at hand.

How you process the answers also matters. It's natural, as conversations unfold, to assume you understand what's being said. But what people hear is biased by their expertise and experiences. So it's important to train people to check whether they're truly getting their colleagues' meaning, by using language like "This is what I'm hearing—did I miss anything?" or "Can you help me fill in the gaps?" or "I think what you said means the project is on track. Is that correct?"

Finally, periodic temperature taking is needed to examine the collaborative process itself. The only way to find out how others are experiencing a project or relationship is by asking questions such as "How do you think the project is going?" and "What could we do to work together more effectively?"

3. Get People to See the World Through Others' Eyes

Leaders shouldn't just encourage employees to be curious about different groups and ask questions about their thinking and practices; they should also urge their people to actively consider others' points of view. People from different organizational groups don't see things the same way. Studies (including research on barriers to successful product innovation that the management professor Deborah Dougherty conducted at Wharton) consistently reveal that this leads to misunderstandings in interface work. It's vital, therefore, to help people learn how to take the perspectives of others. One of us, Amy, has done research showing that ambitious cross-industry innovation projects succeed when diverse participants discover how to do this. New Songdo, a project to build a city from scratch in South Korea that launched a decade ago, provides an instructive example. Early in the effort, project leaders brought together architects, engineers, planners, and environmental experts and helped them integrate their expertise in a carefully crafted learning process designed to break down barriers between disciplines. Today, in striking contrast to other "smart" city projects, New Songdo is 50% complete and has 30,000 residents, 33,000 jobs, and emissions that are 70% lower than those of other developments its size.

In a study of jazz bands and Broadway productions, Brian Uzzi of Northwestern University found that leaders of successful teams had an unusual ability to assume other people's viewpoints. These leaders could speak the multiple "languages" of their teammates. Other research has shown that when members of a diverse team proactively take the perspectives of others, it enhances the positive effect of information sharing and increases the team's creativity.

Creating a culture that fosters this kind of behavior is a senior leadership responsibility. Psychological research suggests that while most people are *capable* of taking others' perspectives, they are rarely *motivated* to do so. Leaders can provide some motivation by emphasizing to their teams how much the integration of diverse expertise enhances new value creation. But a couple of other tactics will help:

Organize cross-silo dialogues

Instead of holding one-way information sessions, leaders should set up cross-silo discussions that help employees see the world through the eyes of customers or colleagues in other parts of the company. The goal is to get everyone to share knowledge and work on synthesizing that diverse input into new solutions. This happens best in face-to-face meetings that are carefully structured to allow people time to listen to one another's thinking. Sometimes the process includes customers; one consulting firm we know started to replace traditional meetings, at which the firm conveyed information to clients, with a workshop format designed to explore questions and develop solutions in *collaboration* with them. The new format gives both the clients and the consultants a chance to learn from each other.

One of the more thoughtful uses of cross-silo dialogue is the "focused event analysis" (FEA) at Children's Minnesota. In an FEA people from the health system's different clinical and operational groups come together after a failure, such as the administration of the wrong medication to a patient. One at a time participants offer their take on what happened; the goal is to carefully document multiple perspectives *before* trying to identify a cause. Often participants are surprised to learn how people from other groups saw the incident. The assumption underlying the FEA is that most failures have not one root cause but many. Once the folks involved have a multifunctional picture of the contributing factors, they can alter procedures and systems to prevent similar failures.

Hire for curiosity and empathy

You can boost your company's capacity to see the world from different perspectives by bringing on board people who relate to and sympathize with the feelings, thoughts, and attitudes of others. Southwest Airlines, which hires fewer than 2% of all applicants, selects people with empathy and enthusiasm for customer service, evaluating them through behavioral interviews ("Tell me about a time when . . .") and team interviews in which candidates are observed interacting.

4. Broaden Your Employees' Vision

You can't lead at the interfaces if you don't know where they are. Yet many organizations unwittingly encourage employees to never look beyond their own immediate environment, such as their function or business unit, and as a result miss out on potential insights employees could get if they scanned more-distant networks. Here are some ways that leaders can create opportunities for employees to widen their horizons, both within the company and beyond it:

Bring employees from diverse groups together on initiatives

As a rule, cross-functional teams give people across silos a chance to identify various kinds of expertise within their organization, map how they're connected or disconnected, and see how the internal knowledge network can be linked to enable valuable collaboration.

At one global consulting firm, the leader of the digital health-care practice used to have its consultants speak just to clients' CIOs and CTOs. But she realized that that "unnecessarily limited the practice's ability to identify opportunities to serve clients beyond IT," she says. So she began to set up sessions with the entire C-suite at clients and brought in consultants from across all her firm's health-care practices—including systems redesign, operations excellence, strategy, and financing—to provide a more integrated look at the firm's health-care innovation expertise.

Those meetings allowed the consultants to discover the connections among the practices in the health-care division, identify the people best positioned to bridge the different practices, and see novel ways to combine the firm's various kinds of expertise to meet clients' needs. That helped the consultants spot value-generating opportunities for services at the interfaces between the practices. The new approach was so effective that, in short order, the leader was asked to head up a new practice that served as an interface across all the practices in the IT division so that she could replicate her success in other parts of the firm.

Urge employees to explore distant networks

Employees also need to be pushed to tap into expertise outside the company and even outside the industry. The domains of human knowledge span science, technology, business, geography, politics, history, the arts, the humanities, and beyond, and any interface between them could hold new business opportunities. Consider the work of the innovation consultancy IDEO. By bringing design techniques from technology, science, and the arts to business, it has been able to create revolutionary products, like the first Apple mouse (which it developed from a Xerox PARC prototype into a commercial offering), and help companies in many industries embrace design thinking as an innovation strategy.

The tricky part is finding the domains most relevant to key business goals. Although many innovations have stemmed from what Abraham Flexner, the founding director of the Institute for

Advanced Study, called "the usefulness of useless knowledge," businesses can ill afford to rely on open-ended exploratory search alone. To avoid this fate, leaders can take one of two approaches:

A *top-down approach* works when the knowledge domains with high potential for value creation have already been identified. For example, a partner in an accounting firm who sees machine learning as key to the profession's future might have an interested consultant or analyst in her practice take online courses or attend industry conferences about the technology and ask that person to come back with ideas about its implications. The partner might organize workshops in which the junior employee shares takeaways from the learning experiences and brainstorms, with experienced colleagues, potential applications in the firm.

A *bottom-up approach* is better when leaders have trouble determining which outside domains the organization should connect with—a growing challenge given the speed at which new knowledge is being created. Increasingly, leaders must rely on employees to identify and forge connections with far-flung domains. One approach is to crowdsource ideas for promising interfaces—for example, by inviting employees to propose conferences in other industries they'd like to attend, courses on new skill sets they'd like to take, or domain experts they'd like to bring in for workshops. It's also critical to give employees the time and resources to scan external domains and build connections to them.

Breaking Down Silos

In today's economy everyone knows that finding new ways to combine an organization's diverse knowledge is a winning strategy for creating lasting value. But it doesn't happen unless employees have the opportunities and tools to work together productively across silos. To unleash the potential of horizontal collaboration, leaders must equip people to learn and to relate to one another across cultural and logistical divides. The four practices we've just described can help.

Not only is each one useful on its own in tackling the distinct challenges of interface work, but together these practices are mutually enhancing: Engaging in one promotes competency in another. Deploying cultural brokers who build connections across groups gets people to ask questions and learn what employees in other groups are thinking. When people start asking better questions, they're immediately better positioned to understand others' perspectives and challenges. Seeing things from someone else's perspective—walking in his or her moccasins—in turn makes it easier to detect more pockets of knowledge. And network scanning illuminates interfaces where cultural brokers might be able to help groups collaborate effectively.

Over time these practices—none of which require advanced degrees or deep technical smarts—dissolve the barriers that make boundary-crossing work so difficult. When leaders create conditions that encourage and support these practices, collaboration across the interface will ultimately become second nature.

Originally published in May–June 2019. Reprint R1903J

Toward a Racially Just Workplace

by Laura Morgan Roberts and Anthony J. Mayo

"SUCCESS IS TO BE MEASURED not so much by the position that one has reached in life as by the obstacles which [one] has overcome while trying to succeed."

Booker T. Washington, the educator, author, activist, and presidential adviser, wrote those words more than a century ago as a way of encouraging his African-American compatriots—many of them recently emancipated from slavery—to persist in the fight for equal rights and economic opportunities. He was proud of what he and his peers had achieved. He surely believed there was satisfaction in struggling against and surmounting bad odds. And yet we must also assume that he, along with millions of other freedom fighters, wanted future generations of black Americans to suffer fewer hardships. He hoped today's black leaders would find easier paths to success.

Has that dream been realized? Having spent the past 20 years conducting and reviewing research on African-Americans' advancement, particularly in the workplace, and having collected our work and others' into a book, we must report that the answer is partly yes but mostly no.

No doubt, there has been progress. Civil rights laws have been passed and affirmed. Companies are committing to and investing heavily in diversity, because more corporate leaders acknowledge that it makes good business sense. And several black billionaires and CEOs sit on the respective ranking lists.

However, according to both quantitative and qualitative data, working African-Americans—from those laboring in factories and on shop floors to those setting C-suite strategy—still face obstacles to advancement that other minorities and white women don't. They are less likely than their white peers to be hired, developed, and promoted. And their lived experience at work is demonstrably worse even than that of other people of color.

These challenges might, as Washington said, make success sweeter for the few who overcome them. But a huge gap remains between what organizations are saying and doing to promote inclusion and the outcomes we're seeing for many black workers and managers. If leaders want to walk their talk, they must spearhead much more meaningful change. Instead of undervaluing and squandering black talent, they must recognize the resilience, robust sense of self, and growth mindset that, studies show, African-American people—as one of the most historically oppressed groups in the United States—bring to the table. They should work even harder to seek out and support them, from entry-level recruitment to CEO succession.

We have not identified any major company that is doing this well on a broad scale. But research and lessons gleaned from other contexts can point the way forward. In our work with leading management thinkers and practitioners across the country, we have arrived at a four-step strategy to help companies move toward greater and better representation for black leaders. It involves shifting from an exclusive focus on the business case for racial diversity to embracing the moral one, promoting real conversations about race, revamping diversity and inclusion programs, and better managing career development at every stage. Given the increasing importance of purpose and social impact to employees, customers, and other stakeholders, we believe there's no better time to make this transformation. We also believe our framework can be adapted for other marginalized groups in the United States and around the world.

Taking these steps won't be easy; executives will need to think deeply about their ethics and corporate culture and exert extra effort

Idea in Brief

At most large U.S. and multinational organizations, diversity and inclusion have become imperatives, but African-Americans' progress remains slow. Even worse is the lived experience of black employees, who often feel like outsiders—and are tempted to walk out the door. Laura Morgan Roberts and Anthony J. Mayo argue that organizations should take specific steps toward racial justice:

- Shift from an exclusive focus on the most lucrative thing to do to the right thing to do.

- Encourage open conversations about race.

- Revamp diversity and inclusion programs to clarify goals and focus on proactive steps.

- Manage career development across all life stages, from campus recruitment to the consideration of black executives for top jobs.

These steps won't be easy, but maximizing the human potential of everyone in the workplace is the ultimate reward.

for a cause they may not consider central to their business. But the reward will be great: maximizing the human potential of everyone in the workplace.

Underrepresented, Unsupported, Unfulfilled

At most large U.S. and multinational organizations, diversity and inclusion (D&I) has become an imperative. Companies are pushing for minority recruitment, paying for antibias training, and sponsoring nonwhite employees for high-potential leadership-development programs. Research has shown, and a great many executives now understand, that a heterogeneous workforce yields more innovation and better performance than a homogeneous one does.

And yet 55 years after the passage of the Civil Rights Act and decades into these corporate D&I efforts, African-Americans' progress toward top management roles and greater economic well-being and influence remains slow to nonexistent. Let's look first at the demographics.

The Big Idea: Advancing Black Leaders

"Toward a Racially Just Workplace" is the lead article of HBR's **The Big Idea: Advancing Black Leaders.** You can read the rest of the series at hbr.org/blackleaders:

- "The Costs of Code-Switching," by Courtney L. McCluney, Kathrina Robotham, Serenity Lee, Richard Smith, and Myles Durkee
- "The Day-to-Day Work of Diversity and Inclusion," by Paige Cohen and Gretchen Gavett
- "Why So Many Organizations Stay White," by Victor Ray
- "Success Comes from Affirming Your Potential," by Laura Morgan Roberts and Anthony J. Mayo

What the numbers say

Yes, we can point to the rise of several prominent black leaders, from media figures Oprah Winfrey, Robert Johnson, and Jay-Z to financiers Ken Chenault and Robert Smith and sports-stars-turned-businesspeople Serena Williams, Michael Jordan, and LeBron James. Most notably, America elected its first African-descended president, Barack Obama, in 2008 and reelected him in 2012. The number of African-Americans earning bachelor's and graduate degrees continues to increase. And black people account for 12% of the U.S. workforce, close to their 13.4% representation in the general population.

However, in the words of leaders from the Toigo Foundation, a career advancement organization for underrepresented groups, such evidence merely gives us "the illusion of inclusion." In fact, research shows that in the United States, the wealth gap between blacks and others continues to widen; experts predict that black families' median wealth will decrease to $0 by 2050, while that of white families will exceed $100,000. Just 8% of managers and 3.8% of CEOs are black. In the *Fortune* 500 companies, there are currently only three black chief executives, down from a high of 12 in 2002. And at the 16 *Fortune* 500 companies that report detailed demographic data on senior executives and board members, white men account for 85% of those roles.

Black leaders have struggled to make inroads in a variety of influential industries and sectors. At U.S. finance companies, only 2.4% of executive committee members, 1.4% of managing directors, and 1.4% of senior portfolio managers are black. A mere 1.9% of tech executives and 5.3% of tech professionals are African-American. Black representatives and senators account for 9% of the U.S. Congress. The average black partnership rate at U.S. law firms from 2005 to 2016 was 1.8%. Only 7% of U.S. higher education administrators and 8% of nonprofit leaders are black. And just 10% of U.S. businesses are owned by black men and women. As the Toigo Foundation points out, all this has a cascading impact on economic development, housing, jobs, quality of schools and other services, access to education, infrastructure spending, consumer credit, retirement savings, and more.

What it's like at work

Underrepresentation is bad enough. But even worse, according to extensive research, is the lived experience of black employees and managers in the U.S. workplace. African-Americans continue to face both explicit racism—stoked by the rise of white nationalism in the past few years—and subtle racism on the job. In the latter category, University of Utah professor emeritus Arthur Brief points to "aversive" racism (when people avoid those of different races or change their behavior around them) along with "modern" racism (when people believe that because blacks can now compete in the marketplace, they no longer face discrimination). Microagressions—for example, when a white male visitor to an office assumes that a black female executive is a secretary—are also common.

Although companies claim they want to overcome these explicit and implicit biases and hire and promote diverse candidates, they rarely do so in effective ways. When Harvard Business School's emeriti professors David A. Thomas and John Gabarro conducted an in-depth six-year study of leaders in three companies, they found that people of color had to manage their careers more strategically than their white peers did and to prove greater competence before winning promotions. And research by Lynn Perry Wooten, the dean of Cornell University's Dyson School, and Erika Hayes James, the dean of Emory University's Goizueta Business School, shows that black leaders who do rise to the top are disproportionately handed "glass cliff" assignments, which offer nice rewards but carry a greater risk of failure. Other research, such as Duke University professor Ashleigh Rosette's studies of black leaders, has shown widespread racial differences in hiring, performance ratings, promotions, and other outcomes.

There is also an emotional tax associated with being black in the American workplace. Research by the University of Virginia's Courtney McCluney and Catalyst's Dnika Travis and Jennifer Thorpe-Moscon shows that because black employees feel a heightened sense of difference among their mostly white peers, their ability to contribute is diminished. "The sense of isolation, of solitude, can take a toll," one leader told them. "It's like facing each day with a core of uncertainty . . . wondering . . . if the floor you're standing on is concrete or dirt . . . solid or not."

Many black professionals have reported to Toigo that they are expected to be "cultural ambassadors" who address the needs of other black employees, which leaves them doing two jobs: "the official one the person was hired to do, and a second one as champion for members of the person's minority group," as one put it. Across industries, sectors, and functions, they also experience the "diversity fatigue" that arises from constantly engaging in task forces, trainings, and conversations about race as they are tapped to represent their demographic.

And black leaders in particular struggle with feeling inauthentic at work. Research by McGill University's Patricia Faison Hewlin shows that many minorities feel pressured to create "facades of conformity," suppressing their personal values, views, and attributes to fit in with organizational ones. But as Hewlin and her colleague Anna-Maria Broomes found in a survey of 2,226 workers in various industries and corporate settings, African-Americans create these facades more frequently than other minority groups do and feel the inauthenticity more deeply. They might chemically relax (straighten) their hair, conform with coworkers' behavior, "whitewash" their résumés by deleting ethnic-sounding names or companies, hide minority beliefs, and suppress emotions related to workplace racism.

As a result of all the above, black workers feel less supported, engaged, and committed to their jobs than their nonblack peers do, as research from Georgetown University's Ella Washington, Gallup's Ellyn Maese and Shane McFeely, and others has documented. Black managers report receiving less psychosocial support than their white counterparts do. Black employees are less likely than whites or Hispanics to say that their company's mission or purpose makes them feel that their job is important, that their coworkers will do quality work, and that they have opportunities to learn and grow. Black leaders are more likely than white ones to leave their organizations. It's clear that the norms and cultural defaults of leadership in most organizations create an inhospitable environment that leaves even those black employees who have advanced feeling like outsiders—and in some cases pushes them out the door.

Relatively high pay and impressive pedigrees don't help much: According to a survey of diverse professionals with bachelor's or graduate degrees and average annual incomes of $100,000 or more that one of us (Laura) conducted with colleagues at the Partnership, a nonprofit organization specializing in diversity and leadership development, African-Americans report the lowest levels of both manager and coworker support, commitment, and job fit and the highest levels of feeling inauthentic and wanting to leave their jobs. Studies of black Harvard Business School and Harvard Law School graduates have similarly found that matriculating from highly respected institutions does not shield one from obstacles. When surveyed years and even decades after graduating, black Harvard MBAs expressed less satisfaction than their white counterparts with opportunities to do meaningful work, to realize professional accomplishments, and to combine career with personal and family life. "Perhaps it sounds naive, but [coming out of HBS] I did not expect race to have any bearing in my career," one told us. "I was wrong."

Leading Change

As we said earlier, diversity and inclusion efforts have been gaining traction, and workforces are becoming increasingly multiracial. But given the dearth of black leaders, we would like to see companies jump-start their efforts in four ways.

First, move away from the business case and toward a moral one

The dozens of D&I executives we talked to in the course of our research tell us they sometimes feel they've taken the business case for diversity as far as it can go. When Weber Shandwick surveyed 500 chief diversity officers at companies with revenue of $500 million or more, results confirmed that proving that ROI—showing that inclusive teams yield more-creative ideas that appeal to broader customer bases, open new markets, and ultimately drive better performance—is one of the biggest challenges.

The research on this is clear. A 2015 McKinsey report on 366 public companies found that those in the top quartile for ethnic and racial diversity in management were 35% more likely than others to have financial returns above the industry mean. Various studies have shown that teams composed of both white and black people are more likely to focus on facts, carefully process information, and spur innovation when the organizational culture and leadership support learning across differences.

With the right knowledge, skills, and experience, African-American employees and managers can add as much business value as anyone else. They may have greater insights about creating and selling offerings for minority consumer groups that end up appealing to white consumers as well. As one of us (Tony) showed in research with Nitin Nohria, now the dean of Harvard Business School, and Eckerd College's Laura Singleton, some of the most successful black entrepreneurs are those who—in some cases *because* they were marginalized—built companies to serve their same-race peers, particularly in the personal care, media, and fashion arenas. Examples include the 19th-century black-hair-care trailblazer Madam C. J. Walker, Black Entertainment Television's

Robert and Sheila Johnson, and Daymond John, who launched the FUBU clothing line.

So, experts agree that diversity enhances business outcomes when managed well. But given the limited progress African-Americans have made in most of corporate America, it seems clear that the sound business arguments for inclusion are not enough. At many companies, D&I executives still struggle for airtime in the C-suite and for resources that can move their organizations beyond the tokenism of, say, one black executive in the senior ranks. Their business cases don't appear to have been as persuasive as those presented by their marketing, operations, and accounting colleagues, which have a more direct effect on the bottom line.

And in more-progressive companies—ones truly committed to inclusion—a different kind of pushback sometimes occurs: If a team incorporates women, Asians, Latinos, and representatives of the LGBTQ community alongside white men, if it has data geeks and creative types, extroverts and introverts, Harvard MBAs and college dropouts, able-bodied and physically challenged members, isn't it diverse enough? Our answer: not when teams, especially those at the highest levels, leave out the most marginalized group in the United States.

Thus we turn to the moral case. Many in the U.S. business community have begun to push for a more purpose-driven capitalism that focuses not just on shareholder value but also on shared value—benefits that extend to employees, customers, suppliers, and communities. This movement, toward what the University of Toronto's Sarah Kaplan calls the 360° Corporation, wants corporate leaders to consider both the financial and the ethical implications of all their decisions. We believe that one of its pillars should be proportionate representation and wages for black Americans.

Why this group in particular? As the *New York Times*'s excellent 1619 Project highlighted, we are exactly four centuries away from the start of slavery—the kidnapping, forced labor, mistreatment, and often murder of African people—in the United States. And we are just 154 years away from its end. Although discrimination based on race and other factors was outlawed by the Civil Rights Act of 1964, the effects of slavery and the decades of discrimination and disenfranchisement that followed it continue to hold back many descendants of enslaved people (and those from different circumstances who have the same skin color). Alarmingly, racism and racist incidents are on the rise: According to the FBI, the number of hate crimes committed in the United States rose by 17% from 2016 to 2017, marking the third consecutive year of increases.

We also can't forget that a compelling business case can be—and has been—made for all the atrocities listed above. Indeed, when invoked absent humanistic and ethical principles, a "business case" has legitimated exploitative actions throughout history. White landowners argued that the economic welfare of the colonies and the health of a young country depended on keeping black people in chains. White business owners in the Jim Crow South and segregated neighborhoods across the country claimed that sales would suffer if black customers and residents—who in the absence of land and good jobs had amassed little wealth—were allowed in, because that would turn rich white customers away. And white executives have long benefited because people of color with less access to high-quality education and high-wage employment were forced into low-paying commercial and household jobs, from coal mining and call center work to cleaning, cooking, and caregiving.

So the case for racial diversity and the advancement of African-Americans can't be solely about increasing innovation or providing access to and legitimacy in minority markets to maximize revenue and profits. We can't simply ask, "What's the most lucrative thing to do?" We must also ask, "What's the right thing to do?" The imperative should be creating a context in which people of all colors, but especially those who have historically been oppressed, can realize their full potential. This will involve exploring and understanding the racist history that has shaped various groups' access to resources and opportunities and that undergirds contemporary bias. It means emphasizing equity and justice.

How might this work? Starbucks has made some attempts. In the wake of protests following the 2014 fatal shooting of Michael Brown by police in Ferguson, Missouri, the coffee chain announced RaceTogether, which aimed to spark a national conversation about race relations by having baristas write that phrase on customers' cups. The campaign fell flat because it was perceived more as a profit-minded marketing stunt than as a good-faith effort to change the status quo. Subsequent initiatives, perhaps designed with ethics more squarely in mind, have garnered a more positive response. In 2015 Starbucks launched a hiring program to recruit disadvantaged youths, including African-Americans; in 2017 it expanded that program and added one to recruit refugees; and after a racially charged incident at one of its cafés in 2018, it closed all its U.S. cafés for a day of employee antibias training. Consider, too, Nike's decision to launch a marketing campaign headlined by Colin Kaepernick, the NFL quarterback who failed to get picked up by a team after he began kneeling during the national anthem to protest the unfair treatment of African-Americans. The campaign created a backlash among anti-Kaepernick consumers and a #BoycottNike hashtag, but the sports apparel brand stood by its tagline: "Believe in something. Even if it means sacrificing everything." We applaud these steps and hope organizations will go even further in learning how to practice racial inclusion in their workplaces.

Some organizations have invoked the moral case for action in other contexts. Think of how Patagonia supports environmental protections by committing to donate either 1% of sales or 10% of profits (whichever is larger) to advocacy groups. And recall that Dick's Sporting Goods pulled assault weapons and high-capacity magazines from its stores following the Parkland, Florida, school shooting, even though it projected—accurately—that the move would mean a $250 million hit to sales. (It's important to note that over the long term, none of those companies suffered from their choices.)

Such stances take courage. But by combining the business case and the moral one, leaders can make a more powerful argument for supporting black advancement.

Second, encourage open conversations about race

As Dartmouth College's Ella Bell and the University of Pretoria's Stella Nkomo note in the introduction to our book, "Organizations are in society, not apart from it." And although President Obama's election brought some talk of a post-racial era in the United States, the stories and statistics that have come out in the past few years show that racism still exists, which means that race still matters and needs to be discussed, candidly and frequently, in the workplace.

Those conversations will not immediately feel comfortable. Research shows that although many people are happy to talk about "diversity" or "inclusion," their enthusiasm drops significantly when the subject is "race." Most of us don't like to think very hard about where minorities sit and what power they wield (or don't) within our organizations—much less discuss it. When we examine who has been excluded in what ways over what period of time, the concept of white privilege might come up. And majority-group employees might express concerns about reverse discrimination. (According to an Ernst & Young study of 1,000 U.S. workers, one-third of respondents said that a corporate focus on diversity has overlooked white men.) Charged topics like these can provoke resentment, anger, and shame. But we need real exchanges about them if we want to dispel the notion that corporations are pure meritocracies and to ensure that everyone feels heard, supported, and authentic at work.

Senior leaders—most of whom are white men—must set the tone. Why? In one survey, nearly 40% of black employees said they feel it is *never* acceptable to speak out about experiences of bias—a silence that can become corrosive. Another study showed that among black professionals who aspire to senior leadership positions, the most frequently adopted strategy is to avoid talking about race or other issues of inequality, for fear of being labeled an agitator. Other research has indicated that the only CEOs and lower-level managers not penalized for championing diversity are white men.

To create a culture of psychological safety and pave the way for open communication will require a top-down directive and modeling through informal and formal discussions in which people are asked to share ideas, ask questions, and address issues without fear of reprisal. Managers down the line will need training in encouraging and guiding such exchanges, including inviting black employees and leaders to share their experiences—the good, the bad, and the ugly. Participants should be trained to prepare for such conversations by reflecting on their own identities and the comments and situations that trigger strong emotions in them. As detailed by Columbia University's Valerie Purdie-Greenaway and the University of Virginia's Martin Davidson, the goal is to shift the entire organization to a racial-learning orientation.

Again, a movement from another context—#MeToo—sheds light on how to do so. Revelations of abuse and harassment and the outpouring of women's stories that followed, many about incidents that happened in the workplace, forced corporate leaders to focus on those issues. Bad actors were fired, women felt empowered to speak up, and awareness of gender discrimination increased. Although #BlackLivesMatter has had similar success highlighting and sparking discussions around police brutality, there is no #BlackLivesAtWork. There should be.

We see some positive signs on this front. Over the past few years several prominent leaders, including PwC's Tim Ryan, Interpublic Group's Michael Roth, Kaiser Permanente's Bernard Tyson, and AT&T's Randall Stephenson, have initiated companywide discussions of race. For example, PwC brought in Mellody Hobson, president and co-CEO of Ariel Investments and a prominent African-American leader, to talk to employees about being "color-brave" instead of "color-blind" at work, and it has offered guides for continuing the discussion. At Morgan Stanley, global head of D&I Susan Reid has promoted intimate conversations about race in networking groups and an hour-long forum on race in the current social climate. The latter was moderated by the company's vice chairman and featured its chief marketing officer, its head of prime brokerage, and a *Fortune* reporter who covers racial issues; it was attended by 1,500 employees, and videos of the event were shared across the firm. Greenaway and Davidson also point to a mostly white male financial services firm that instituted Know Us, a program of small-group cross-race dialogues on racially relevant topics.

Over time these conversations will start to happen informally and organically in groups and among individuals at all levels of an organization, deepening interpersonal cross-race relationships. In one consulting company cited by Greenaway and Davidson, nonblack employees started a book club open to all but focused on black writers; the group has visited African-American museums and historical sites. One-on-one interactions can be even more meaningful, as the psychologist colleagues Karen Samuels (who is white) and Kathryn Fraser (who is black) describe. "It was important to name our racial and cultural differences and to examine how my perspective was naive regarding her reality," Samuels explains.

Third, revamp D&I programs

Any corporate diversity and inclusion program is better than none, but most that exist today are not designed to sustain a focus on racial equity. Many are siloed within the HR department, lack C-suite support, or are given to women or people of color to manage in addition to their day jobs. Some are more show than go, resting on philosophical statements about inclusion rather than outlining concrete steps for advancing nonwhites. Others limit their efforts to antibias and cultural competence training—preempting problems but, again, not propelling anyone forward. Most take a broad-brush approach to diversity, attempting to serve all minorities plus white women, LGBTQ employees, and those who are neurodiverse or disabled and offering uniform training and leadership development that ignore historical patterns of exclusion, marginality, and disadvantage for each group. They might focus too heavily on recruitment and retention—filling the pipeline and high-potential groups with black employees but failing to support them past middle-management roles. Most troubling, as Courtney McCluney and San Francisco State University's Verónica Rabelo have shown, a significant portion of D&I programs try to "manage blackness"—that is, impose "desirable" and "professional" (read: white) norms and expectations on rising African-American stars, thus preserving rather than shifting the status quo. They train black executives to fit into the existing organizational culture rather than encourage them to broaden it by bringing their true and most productive selves to work.

How can we improve such programs? By tackling their shortcomings one by one. Here are several steps organizations can take.

- Give D&I sustained C-suite support and recognize and reward the people who contribute to its initiatives—for example, by having your chief diversity officer report directly to the CEO and tracking inclusion initiative participation in performance reviews and promotion and pay raise discussions.

- Equip and invite white men to take up the mantle—say, by bringing them into D&I programs and assigning some of them to leadership roles.

- Challenge those running D&I efforts to set clear goals for how representation, organizational networks, and access to resources should change across functions and levels over time and how black employees' perceptions, engagement, and well-being should improve, and then measure the efforts' effectiveness with data analysis and qualitative surveys.

- Shift from preventative measures, such as antibias training, to proactive ones, such as upping the number of black candidates considered for open positions and stretch roles.

- Abandon one-size-fits-all and color-blind leadership-development practices in favor of courses and coaching tailored to specific groups—or better yet, adopt personalized plans that recognize the multifaceted nature of each individual.

- Help black employees and rising leaders throughout their careers, including teaching managers the skills they need to support D&I efforts.

- Stop asking black employees to blend in; instead, emphasize the value of a workplace that embraces all styles and behaviors.

In sum, D&I needs to be an ethos that permeates the entire organization, championed not just by the HR department but by everyone, and especially managers, so that its importance is clear. The Toigo Foundation's leaders draw a parallel between this idea and the total quality management movement of the 1980s, which, with top-down support and the establishment of key performance indicators, became a pervasive way of working and thinking that filtered down to every function and level.

Few companies to date have taken diversity and inclusion that far. But some are moving in the right direction, including JPMorgan Chase, which in 2016 launched a board- and CEO-supported Advancing Black Leaders strategy—staffed and managed separately from other D&I initiatives—focused on filling the firm's pipeline with black talent and retaining and promoting those workers. SAP's Black Employee Network helped launch its partnership with Delaware State University through Project Propel, which offers tech training and skills development to students from historically black colleges and universities (HBCUs), with the goal of building an employee pipeline. The Network also encouraged SAP to sponsor Silicon Valley's Culture Shifting Weekend, which brings together more than 200 African-American and Hispanic executives, entrepreneurs, innovators, and social impact leaders to discuss diversifying the tech industry. Pfizer tracks numerous D&I metrics and notes that 21% of its workforce—21,000 people—are actively involved in its D&I efforts.

Finally, manage career development across all life stages
African-Americans today are securing good university educations in record numbers. HBCUs, in particular, create a sizable pipeline of young talent for organizations to tap into. Companies can, of course, step up their campus recruiting efforts, but efforts to advance black leaders must extend far beyond that.

If more African-Americans are to rise through the ranks, robust— and careful—investment in retention and development is required. Research by the University of Georgia's Kecia Thomas and colleagues has shown that many black women get this kind of support early in their careers, but it comes with a price: They are treated like "pets" whom white leaders are happy to groom, but the further they progress, the more that favored status begins to undermine them. Those who reject the pet identity, meanwhile, are perceived as threatening and face hostility and distancing from coworkers.

Mentoring is useful, and our study of black HBS graduates shows that they were more likely than their white peers to have been formally assigned to mentors. But they derived less value from the relationship and said that informal mentorship—having senior executives (white or minority) connect with them naturally through work groups or common interests—was more effective. "A mentor helps you navigate the power structure of the firm, especially when there is no one in senior management who looks like you," one study participant told us.

Early in their careers, black employees need safe spaces to grow and develop and to experience authentic failures and successes without being subsumed in narratives of racial limitation. Managers and mentors can provide the necessary cover. We found that the black Harvard MBAs who did reach top management positions (13% of women, 19% of men) had been bolstered by networks of supporters.

Sponsorship—that is, recommending black employees for promotions and stretch assignments—is even more important. Other key factors that have propelled black Harvard MBAs into senior executive roles are line or general management experience and global assignments. With many qualified and ambitious people vying for such opportunities, politics often plays a role. So African-Americans need more influential people in their corners, pressing their cases to decision-makers.

Candid feedback early on is also critical. This doesn't mean pushing protégés to assimilate (to look and act "more white"); as we've shown, that's counterproductive. It should focus on identifying and enhancing their unique strengths, overcoming skill or knowledge weaknesses, and positioning them to realize their full potential.

At later stages of their careers, black executives should be seriously considered for high-stakes and high-profile positions and supported in the pursuit of outside interests, such as board seats, that enhance visibility. And while taking care not to tokenize but rather to create opportunities for multiple candidates, organizations can highlight those executives as role models who redefine norms of leadership and can encourage them to pass that baton by transferring connections and endorsements, sharing wisdom through storytelling, and creating opportunities for the next generation to assume senior roles. Needs differ by career stage, a fact that most published models of diversity and inclusion do not address but that is embedded in impactful programs such as the Toigo Foundation, the Partnership, and the Executive Leadership Council.

Despite antidiscrimination laws and increasing corporate investment in diversity efforts, race continues to be a major barrier to advancement in the U.S. workplace. We are far from realizing the principles of equal opportunity and meritocracy. Rather than looking to the few black leaders who have succeeded as exemplars of exceptionalism who have beaten almost insurmountable odds, we must learn from their insights and experiences along with the experiences of those who didn't make it to the top. Perhaps more important, we need to understand why existing inclusion initiatives have made so little difference. If organizations really want a representative workforce that includes more than one or two black leaders, their approach must change.

Our hope is that once companies understand the reality of the black experience, they will embrace and champion policies and programs that actually help to level the playing field—and that where there aren't yet best practices, they will begin the conversations and experiments that will lead to them. This will be hard and often uncomfortable work. But we believe it's worth it, not only for African-Americans but also for the many other underrepresented or marginalized groups. Now more than ever before, organizations and society should strive to benefit from the experiences, knowledge, and skills of all, not just a few. And while government policies can help, we believe that corporate leaders can have a much more powerful and immediate impact. As then-Senator Obama said in 2008, *"Change will not come if we wait for some other person or if we wait for some other time. We are the ones we've been waiting for. We are the change that we seek."*

The Day-to-Day Work of Diversity and Inclusion

A conversation with Airbnb's Melissa Thomas-Hunt on creating a culture in which black employees can thrive. *by Paige Cohen and Gretchen Gavett*

Most leaders of U.S. companies know that attracting diverse employees is good business. In response, the prevalence of diversity and inclusion professionals has increased and diversity trainings have become the norm. Yet these efforts, at least in their current forms, aren't boosting the representation of African-Americans in organizations and in leadership roles. What needs to change to create racially inclusive workplaces? And how can managers be the catalysts?

Dr. Melissa Thomas-Hunt is Airbnb's head of global diversity and belonging, and has been working in the diversity and inclusion space for decades, both at organizations and in academia. She spoke with us about how diversity efforts can do a better job of addressing the needs of black workers. She emphasized that there's no quick fix: "Big wins will come from interrogating seemingly mundane practices and processes, and holding managers and leaders accountable for progress toward your organization's aspirations."

An edited version of our conversation with Dr. Thomas-Hunt is below.

How do you design a diversity and inclusion program for black workers to reach leadership positions—and succeed in them?

Creating a work environment in which black employees can thrive requires deliberate, sustained efforts focused primarily in three areas: data and numbers, company culture, and day-to-day people management.

49

We know that numbers matter because who you hire, and at what level, directly affects the overarching narrative of what is normal and accepted in your organization. For example, if the majority of your leadership roles are occupied by white workers, you are sending the message that this group has the most potential to contribute at high levels. To change this narrative, as a first step, companies need to put more effort into increasing their pipeline of black workers.

To be clear, it's no easy feat getting black employees into an organization—and this is true globally for members of the black diaspora living in places in which they are the minority. Historical artifacts of power and privilege create all kinds of roadblocks for black people. Even when economics and levels of education are comparable, social capital—or the networks people need to gain access to opportunities—may be less available to black professionals than to their white counterparts.

So companies need to start putting more systems into place, whether through HR or recruiters, that will help them identify, attract, and hire black talent—including senior talent into critical leadership roles. But this alone is not enough. Organizations also need to make sure that the black employees they are hiring into lower-level positions are being given opportunities that set them up for success and growth. This means undergoing fundamental shifts in the cultures they create. Black employees need to enter generative work environments—ones that allow all people to grow, develop, and flourish, and ones that signal they are valued. Without these, there will be a revolving door of black talent who arrive excited, energized, and ready to contribute and leave feeling unseen and demoralized.

How can you make this culture change happen?

Though culture change is hard, and the path to it seems murky, we do know that managers are the front line. They're the ones with the power to make employees feel safe enough to contribute their knowledge and perspectives. Managers have the ability to build relationships across difference through their access to other team members and leaders. And managers can use their status to provide growth opportunities to black workers through committed sponsorship efforts and by communicating their value—including their expertise, potential, and accomplishments—to others.

Real culture change will start when managers learn how to do this, and it will require a top-down approach. Companies need to make it clear that a great supervisor is someone who creates an environment in which a diverse array of people can succeed. HR professionals need to be empowered to help managers advance inclusive behaviors and eliminate those that erode inclusion, belonging, and engagement. Resources need to be put toward training managers to understand the ways in which their own identities impact the way they engage with others. When situations arise in which black employees are experiencing microaggressions or outright discrimination, managers should know how to properly address the issues and escalate if necessary.

Organizations also need to create cultures of curiosity where people are in a constant state of discovery, learning about themselves and others. Managers can help make this happen by regularly asking their employees what they need. Holding regular check-ins with each employee is a good way for managers to demonstrate genuine interest in their team's well-being and build a foundation of trust. They should use this time to ask people if they feel supported and safe enough to contribute on a regular basis. This time will also help managers troubleshoot any issues that come up and understand their team members and aspirations, as well as how they can help them get where they want to go.

Lastly, managers should be expected to provide specific, actionable feedback to all employees and push past any hesitations they have about how that feedback will land—a fear that often stops white managers from giving black employees critical feedback. Like everyone else, black employees need honest feedback in order to grow and to get access to leadership opportunities down the line.

At some companies, talking about race consists of one formal conversation a year. How can leaders encourage more frequent discussions?

Conversations about race at work are challenging to have, or even begin, when the people involved don't have a positive relationship. That's why, at regular intervals, your employees should be encouraged to spend time with team members who appear to be different than themselves, or peers whom they do not know well. Remember that people must choose to create space for building relationships before they feel comfortable having hard conversations when racially charged situations do arise. So it's best to start building those relationships now. When opportunities for discussions surrounding race or ethnicity do come up, those participating will be more likely to assume positive intent. For the conversation to be productive, both parties need to agree that missteps will happen, and demonstrate a genuine interest in one another's experiences and perspectives.

How can you get leaders and managers on board with all of these suggestions?

Organizations need to take every opportunity to communicate what is expected of their leaders. It's not the organization's job to change attitudes. But it is their job to weave their values into the processes and practices that reinforce company culture, making sure that everyone—from individual contributors to those in leadership roles—is demonstrating behaviors that align with them.

Holding people accountable is vital to doing this successfully. If senior leaders espouse a set of values but fail to keep the people who report to them accountable for their actions or inactions, middle and lower managers will have little incentive to uphold those values and will focus instead on the business goals that are being measured. We are humans, and our attitudes are imperfect. That's why providing incentives—such as measuring diversity and inclusion efforts in performance evaluations, linking them to salary increases or other forms of compensation, and giving employees who demonstrate inclusive values public recognition—will help companies establish cultures that reinforce what they stand for. If there is a misalignment between your organization's values and the behaviors your employees exhibit, then your accountability structure is likely misaligned and needs to be rethought.

How will companies know if their diversity and inclusion programs are actually helping black employees? In what ways should they collect feedback and measure progress?

Asking employees how things are going is a good first step. To gain deeper insights, however, companies should take the bold step of analyzing employee engagement data by race and ethnicity. This is not often done because of the fear of what might be discovered, and if organizations don't look at their data by subgroup, they can easily claim that they have no knowledge of subgroup differences. Failure to measure engagement by subgroup can be perceived by black employees, and other racial or ethnic minorities, as disinterest in truly understanding the way their lived experience may diverge from others in the organization. This data should be shared and discussed internally. Where divergences in experience exist, companies must take a deep dive to understand and resolve the source of the discrepancy.

Where do you see the biggest disconnects between research and practice? And where have you seen the most promising connections?

In organizations, the degree to which we promote awareness of our unconscious biases is often held up as the solution to all the challenges that accompany diversity and inclusion efforts. But in reality, research shows that awareness can actually increase the problematic behavior we are trying to change. This is because if we know that everyone is biased—which we are—we become less inclined to work against our own biases. We do what others do.

You've been working in inclusion for a long time. What's changed since you started? What remains stubbornly the same? And what makes you the most optimistic about the future?

More organizations recognize that they have a problem with inclusion and are committing to making changes than they were 20 years ago. I'm seeing more companies devote resources to forming diversity and inclusion programs, and hiring professionals to spearhead those efforts. There are also communities of practitioners and academics working together to identify and test best practices, whereas before, researchers and those responsible for implementing solutions rarely talked to one another, and they certainly didn't work collaboratively on challenges.

But many organizations still want quick fixes. They are impatient for better outcomes and sometimes take shortcuts. Today, certain programs still focus on "fixing" black employees as opposed to fixing organizational biases. Others showcase one-off diversity and inclusion efforts, such as showy, expensive conferences with a diverse array of speakers, yet fail to yield sustainable gains for black employees because they don't actually examine the day-to-day practices that may undermine black employee advancement. Additionally, people remain concerned about how diversity and inclusion efforts will affect their career outcomes, and outcomes of others like themselves, if those who are historically underrepresented are given new forms of access and more developmental support.

If you had one message for other diversity and inclusion executives, what would it be?

Moving the needle on inclusion is hard. We are asking individuals to do things differently when they feel like they are already overwhelmed. Successful efforts require a deep commitment to sustained effort and offers of assistance to employees in changing their behaviors. Big wins will come from interrogating seemingly mundane practices and processes, and holding managers and leaders accountable for progress toward your organization's aspirations.

Originally published in November 2019. Reprint BG1906

The Age of Continuous Connection

by Nicolaj Siggelkow and Christian Terwiesch

A SEISMIC SHIFT IS UNDER WAY. Thanks to new technologies that enable frequent, low-friction, customized digital interactions, companies today are building much deeper ties with customers than ever before. Instead of waiting for customers to come to them, firms are addressing customers' needs the moment they arise—and sometimes even earlier. It's a win-win: Through what we call *connected strategies,* customers get a dramatically improved experience, and companies boost operational efficiencies and lower costs.

Consider the MagicBands that Disney World issues all its guests. These small wristbands, which incorporate radio-frequency-identification technology, allow visitors to enter the park, get priority access to rides, pay for food and merchandise, and unlock their hotel rooms. But the bands also help Disney locate guests anywhere in the park and then create customized experiences for them. Actors playing Disney characters, for example, can personally greet guests passing by ("Hey, Sophia! Happy seventh birthday!"). Disney can encourage people to visit attractions with idle capacity ("Short lines at Space Mountain right now!"). Cameras on various rides can automatically take photographs of guests, which Disney can use to create personalized memory books for them, without their ever having to pose for a picture.

Similarly, instead of just selling textbooks, McGraw-Hill Education now offers customized learning experiences. As students use the company's electronic texts to read and do assignments, digital technologies track their progress and feed data to their teachers and to the company. If someone is struggling with an assignment, her teacher will find out right away, and McGraw-Hill will direct the student to a chapter or video offering helpful explanations. Nike, too, has gotten into the game. It can now connect with customers daily, through a wellness system that includes chips embedded in shoes, software that analyzes workouts, and a social network that provides advice and support. That new model has allowed the company to transform itself from a maker of athletic gear into a purveyor of health, fitness, and coaching services.

It's easy to see how Disney, McGraw-Hill, and Nike have used approaches like these to stay ahead of the competition. Many other companies are taking steps to develop their own connected strategies by investing substantially in data gathering and analytics. That's great, but a lot of them are now awash in so much data that they're overwhelmed and struggling to cope. How can managers think clearly and systematically about what to do next? What are the best ways to use all this new information to better connect with customers?

In our research we've identified four effective connected strategies, each of which moves beyond traditional modes of customer interaction and represents a fundamentally new business model. We call them *respond to desire, curated offering, coach behavior,* and *automatic execution.* What's innovative here is not the technologies these strategies incorporate but the ways that companies deploy those technologies to develop continuous relationships with customers.

Below, we'll define these new connected strategies and explore how you can make the most of the ones you choose to adopt. But first let's take stock of the old model they're leaving behind.

Buy What We Have

Most companies still interact with customers only episodically, after customers identify their needs and seek out products or services to meet them. You might call this model *buy what we have.* In it

Idea in Brief

The Old Approach

Companies used to interact with customers only episodically, when customers came to them.

The New Approach

Today, thanks to new technologies, companies can address customers' needs the moment they arise—and sometimes even earlier. With connected strategies, firms

can build deeper ties with customers and dramatically improve their experiences.

The Upshot

Companies need to make continuous connection a fundamental part of their business models. They can do so with four strategies: respond to desire, curated offering, coach behavior, and automatic execution.

---

companies work hard to provide high-quality offerings at a competitive price and base their marketing and operations on the assumption that they'll engage only fleetingly with their customers.

Here's a typical buy-what-we-have experience: One Tuesday, working from home, David is halfway through printing a batch of urgent letters when his toner cartridge runs out. It's maddening. He *really* doesn't have time for this. Grumbling, he hunts around for his keys, gets into his car, and drives 15 minutes to the nearest office supply store. There he wanders the aisles looking for the toner section, which turns out to be an entire wall of identical-looking cartridges. After scanning the options and hoping that he recalls his printer model correctly, he finds the cartridge he needs, but only in a multipack, which is expensive. He sets off in search of a staff member who might know if the store has any single cartridges, and eventually he locates a manager, who disappears into the back of the store to check.

Much time passes. When the manager at last returns, it's to report regretfully that the store is sold out of single cartridges. Because he has to get his letters done, David decides to buy the multipack. He grabs one and heads to the checkout counter to pay, only to find himself waiting in a long line. When he finally gets home, an hour or two later, he's not a happy guy.

We find it helpful to break the traditional customer journey into three distinct stages: *recognize,* when the customer becomes aware of a need; *request,* when he or she identifies a product or service that would satisfy this need and turns to a company to meet it; and *respond,* when the customer experiences how the company delivers the product or service. At each of these stages, David suffered a lot of discomfort, but at no point along the way did the toner company have any way of learning about his discomfort or alleviating it. Company and customer were poorly connected throughout, and both parties suffered.

It doesn't have to play out that way. Each of our four connected strategies could have helped improve David's customer experience at one or more of the stages and helped the company strengthen its business.

Let's explore specifically what each strategy entails.

Respond to Desire

This strategy involves providing customers with services and products they've requested—and doing so as quickly and seamlessly as possible. The essential capabilities here are operational: fast delivery, minimal friction, flexibility, and precise execution. Customers who enjoy being in the driver's seat tend to like this strategy.

To provide a good respond-to-desire experience, companies need to listen carefully to what customers want and make the buying process easy. In many cases, what matters most to customers is the amount of energy they have to expend—the less, the better!

That's certainly what David wanted in his search for a toner cartridge. So let's imagine a respond-to-desire strategy that might serve him well in the future.

Say that upon realizing that he needs a replacement, David goes online to his favorite retailer, types in his printer model, and with just a click or two makes a same-day order for the correct cartridge. His credit card number and address are already stored in the system, so the whole process takes just a minute or two. A few hours later his doorbell rings, and he has exactly what he needs.

Speed is critical in a lot of respond-to-desire situations. Users of Lyft and Uber want cars to arrive promptly. Health care patients want the ability to connect at any time of day or night with their providers. Retail customers want the products they order online to arrive as quickly as possible—a desire that Amazon has famously focused on satisfying, in the process redefining how it interacts with customers. Years ago it set up a "one click" process for ordering and payment, and more recently it has gone even further than that. Today you can give Alexa a command to order a particular product, and she'll take care of the rest of the customer journey for you. That's responding to desire.

Curated Offering

With this strategy, companies get actively involved in helping customers at an earlier stage of the customer journey: after the customers have figured out what they need but before they've decided how to fill that need. Executed properly, a curated-offering strategy not only delights customers but also generates efficiency benefits for companies, by steering customers toward products and services that firms can easily provide at the time. The key capability here is a personalized recommendation process. Customers who value advice—but still want to make the final decision—like this approach.

How might a curated-offering strategy serve David? Consider this scenario: He goes online to order his toner cartridge, and the site automatically suggests the correct one on the basis of what he has bought before. That spares him the hassle of finding the model number of his printer and figuring out which cartridge he needs. So now he just orders what the site suggests, and a few hours later, when his doorbell rings, he's had his needs smoothly and easily met.

Blue Apron and similar meal-kit providers have very effectively adopted the curated-offering strategy. This differentiates them from Instacart and many of the other grocery delivery services that have emerged in recent years, all of which are guided by a "you order, we deliver" principle—in other words, a respond-to-desire strategy. The Instacart approach might suit you better than spending time in a supermarket checkout line, but it doesn't relieve you of the burden of hunting for recipes and creating shopping lists of ingredients. Nor does it prevent you from overbuying when you do your shopping. Blue Apron helps on all those fronts, by presenting you with personally tailored offerings, creating an experience that many people find is more convenient, fun, and healthful than what they would choose on their own.

Coach Behavior

Both of the previous two strategies require customers to identify their needs in a timely manner, which (being human) we're not always good at. Coach-behavior strategies help with this challenge, by proactively reminding customers of their needs and encouraging them to take steps to achieve their goals.

Coaching behavior works best with customers who know they need nudging. Some people want to get in shape but can't stick to a workout regimen. Others need to take medications but are forgetful. In these situations a company can watch over customers and help them. Knowledge of a customer's needs might come from information that the person has previously shared with the firm or from observing the behavior of many customers. The essential capabilities involved are a deep understanding of customer needs ("What does the customer really want to achieve?") and the ability to gather and interpret rich contextual data ("What has the customer done or not done up to this point? Can she now enact behaviors that will get her closer to her goal?").

Here's what a coach-behavior strategy for David might look like: Perhaps the printer itself tracks the number of pages it has generated since David last changed the toner and sends that information back to the manufacturer, which knows that he will soon need a new cartridge. So it might email him a reminder to reorder. At the same time, it might encourage him to run the cleaning function on his printer—a suggestion that will help him avoid later inconveniences. Coached in this way, David will have his new printer cartridge before the old one runs out; he'll lose almost no time in replacing it; and he'll have a clean printer that performs at its best.

To implement coach-behavior approaches well, a company needs to receive information constantly from its customers so that it doesn't miss the right moment to suggest action. The technical challenge in this sort of relationship lies in enabling cheap and reliable two-way communication with customers. Traditionally, this had been difficult, but it's getting easier all the time. The advent of wearable devices, for example, allows health care companies to hover digitally over customers around the clock, constantly monitoring how they're doing.

Nike's new business model incorporates coach-behavior strategies. By making its customers part of virtual running clubs and tracking their runs, the company knows when it's time for their next workout, and through its app it can offer them audio training guides and plans. This kind of timely and personal connection builds trust and encourages customers to think of Nike as a health-and-fitness coach rather than just a shoe manufacturer, which in turn means that when the company's app nudges them to run, they're more likely to do it. This serves customers well, because it keeps them motivated and in shape. And it serves Nike well, of course, because customers who run more buy more shoes.

Automatic Execution

All the strategies we've discussed so far require customer involvement. But this last strategy allows companies to meet the needs of customers even before they've become aware of those needs.

In an automatic-execution strategy, customers authorize a company to take care of something, and from that point on the company handles everything. The essential elements here are strong trust, a rich flow of information from the customers, and the ability to use it to flawlessly anticipate what they want. The customers most open to automatic execution are comfortable having data stream constantly from their devices to companies they buy from and have faith that those companies will use their data to fulfill their needs at a reasonable price and without compromising their privacy.

Here's how automatic execution might work for David. When he buys his printer, he authorizes the manufacturer to remotely monitor his ink level and send him new toner cartridges whenever it gets low. From then on, the onus is on the company to manage his needs, and David is spared several hassles: recognizing that he's low on toner, figuring out how to get more, and buying it. Instead, he just goes about his business. When the time is right, his doorbell will ring, and he'll have exactly what he needs.

The growing internet of things is making all sorts of automatic execution possible. David's printer cartridge scenario isn't just hypothetical: Both HP and Brother already have programs that ship replacement toner to customers whenever their printers send out a "low ink" signal. Soon our refrigerators, sensing that we're almost out of milk, will be able to order more for delivery by tomorrow morning—but naturally only after checking our calendar to make sure we're not going on a vacation and wouldn't need milk after all.

Automatic execution will make people's lives easier and in some cases will even save lives. Consider fall-detection sensors, the small medical devices worn by many seniors. Initially, the companies who made them did so using the respond-to-desire model. If an elderly person who was wearing one fell and needed help, she could press a button that activated a distress call. That was good, but it didn't work if someone was too incapacitated to press the button. Now, though, internet-connected wearable technologies allow health care companies to monitor patients constantly in real time, which means people don't need to actively request assistance if and when they're in distress. Imagine a bracelet that monitors vital signs and uses an accelerometer to detect falls. If a person wearing the bracelet slips, tumbles down the basement stairs, and is knocked unconscious, the bracelet's sensor will immediately detect the emergency and summon help. That's automatic execution.

We're excited about automatic execution, but we want to stress that we don't see it as the best solution to all problems—or for all customers. People differ in the degree to which they feel comfortable sharing data and in having the companies serving them act on that data. One family might be delighted to receive an automatically

Which connected strategies should you use?

Connected strategy	Description	Key capability	Works best when	Works best for
Respond to desire	Customer expresses what she wants and when	Fast and efficient response to orders	Customers are knowledgeable	Customers who don't want to share too much data and who like to be in control
Curated offering	Firm offers tailored menu of options to customer	Making good personalized recommendations	The uncurated set of options is large and potentially overwhelming	Customers who don't mind sharing some data but want a final say
Coach behavior	Firm nudges customer to act to obtain a goal	Understanding customer needs and ability to gather and interpret rich data	Inertia and biases keep customers from achieving what's best for them	Customers who don't mind sharing personal data and getting suggestions
Automatic execution	Firm fills customer's need without being asked	Monitoring customers and translating incoming data into action	Customer behavior is very predictable and costs of mistakes are small	Customers who don't mind sharing personal data and having firms make decisions for them

generated personal memory book after a visit to Disney World, but another might think it's creepy and invasive. If companies want customers to make a lot of personal data available on an automated and continuous basis, they will need to prove themselves worthy of their customers' trust. They'll need to show customers that they'll safeguard the privacy and security of personal information and that they'll only recommend products and services in good faith. Breaking a customer's trust at this level could mean losing that customer—and possibly many other customers—forever.

A final important point: Given that companies are likely to have customers with different preferences, most firms will have to create a portfolio of connected strategies, which will require them to build a whole new set of capabilities. (See the table "Which connected strategies should you use?") One-size-fits-all usually won't work.

Repeat

Earlier, we mentioned that we like to think of the individual customer journey as having three stages: *recognize, request,* and *respond.* But there's actually a fourth stage—*repeat*—which is fundamental to any connected strategy, because it transforms stand-alone experiences into long-lasting, valuable relationships. It is in this stage that companies learn from existing interactions and shape future ones—and discover how to create a sustainable competitive advantage.

The repeat dimension of a connected strategy helps companies with two forms of learning.

First, it allows a company to get better at matching the needs of an individual customer with the company's existing products and services. Over time and through multiple interactions, Disney sees that a customer seems to like ice cream more than fries, and theater performances more than fast rides—information that then allows the company to create a more enjoyable itinerary for him. McGraw-Hill sees that a student struggles with compound-interest calculations, which lets it direct her attention to material that covers exactly that weakness. Netflix sees that a customer likes political satire, which allows it to make pertinent movie suggestions to her.

Second, in the repeat stage companies can learn at the population level, which helps them make smart adjustments to their portfolios of products and services. If Disney sees that the general demand for frozen yogurt is rising, it can increase the number of stands in its parks that serve frozen yogurt. If McGraw-Hill sees that many students are struggling with compound-interest calculations, it can refine its online module on that topic. If Netflix observes that many viewers like political dramas, it can license or produce new series in that genre.

Both of these loops have positive feedback effects. The better the company understands a customer, the more it can customize its offerings to her. The more delighted she is by this, the more likely she is to return to the company again, thus providing it with even more data. The more data the company has, the better it can customize its offerings. Likewise, the more new customers a company attracts through its superior customization, the better its population-level data is. The better its population data, the more it can create desirable products. The more desirable its products, the more it can attract new customers. And so on. Both learning loops build on themselves, allowing companies to keep expanding their competitive advantage.

Over time these two loops have another very important effect: They allow companies to address more-fundamental customer needs and desires. McGraw-Hill might find out that a customer wants not just to understand financial accounting but also to have a career on Wall Street. Nike might find out that a particular runner is interested not just in keeping fit but also in training to run a first marathon. That knowledge offers opportunities for companies to create an even wider range of services and to develop trusted relationships with customers that become very hard for competitors to disrupt.

We can't tell you where all this is headed, of course. But here's what we know: The age of "buy what we have" is over. If you want to achieve sustainable competitive advantage in the years ahead, connected strategies need to be a fundamental part of your business. This holds true whether you're a start-up trying to break into an existing industry or an incumbent firm trying to defend your market, and whether you deal directly with consumers or operate in a business-to-business setting. The time to think about connected strategies is now, before others in your industry beat you to it.

Originally published in May–June 2019. Reprint R1903C

The Hard Truth about Innovative Cultures

by Gary P. Pisano

A CULTURE CONDUCIVE TO INNOVATION is not only good for a company's bottom line. It also is something that both leaders and employees value in their organizations. In seminars at companies across the globe, I have informally surveyed hundreds of managers about whether they want to work in an organization where innovative behaviors are the norm. I cannot think of a single instance when someone has said "No, I don't." Who can blame them: Innovative cultures are generally depicted as pretty fun. When I asked the same managers to describe such cultures, they readily provided a list of characteristics identical to those extolled by management books: tolerance for failure, willingness to experiment, psychological safety, highly collaborative, and nonhierarchical. And research supports the idea that these behaviors translate into better innovative performance.

But despite the fact that innovative cultures are desirable and that most leaders claim to understand what they entail, they are hard to create and sustain. This is puzzling. How can practices apparently so universally loved—even fun—be so tricky to implement?

The reason, I believe, is that innovative cultures are misunderstood. The easy-to-like behaviors that get so much attention are only one side of the coin. They must be counterbalanced by some tougher and frankly less fun behaviors. A tolerance for failure requires an intolerance for incompetence. A willingness to experiment requires rigorous discipline. Psychological safety requires comfort with brutal candor. Collaboration must be balanced with an individual accountability. And flatness requires strong leadership. Innovative cultures are paradoxical. Unless the tensions created by this paradox are carefully managed, attempts to create an innovative culture will fail.

1. Tolerance for Failure but No Tolerance for Incompetence

Given that innovation involves the exploration of uncertain and unknown terrain, it is not surprising that a tolerance for failure is an important characteristic of innovative cultures. Some of the most highly touted innovators have had their share of failures. Remember Apple's MobileMe, Google Glass, and the Amazon Fire Phone?

And yet for all their focus on tolerance for failure, innovative organizations are intolerant of incompetence. They set exceptionally high performance standards for their people. They recruit the best talent they can. Exploring risky ideas that ultimately fail is fine, but mediocre technical skills, sloppy thinking, bad work habits, and poor management are not. People who don't meet expectations are either let go or moved into roles that better fit their abilities. Steve Jobs was notorious for firing anyone he deemed not up to the task. At Amazon, employees are ranked on a forced curve, and the bottom part of the distribution is culled. Google is known to have a very employee-friendly culture, but it's also one of the hardest places on earth to get a job (each year the company gets more than 2 million applications for about 5,000 positions). It, too, has a rigorous performance management system that moves people into new roles if they are not excelling in their existing ones. At Pixar, movie directors who cannot get projects on track are replaced.

It sounds obvious that companies should set high quality standards for their employees, but unfortunately all too many organizations fall short in this regard. Consider a pharmaceutical company I recently worked with. I learned that one of its R&D groups had not discovered a new drug candidate in more than a decade. Despite the poor performance, senior leaders had made no real changes in the group's management or personnel. In fact, under the company's egalitarian compensation system, the scientists in the group had been receiving approximately the same salaries and bonuses as scientists in much more productive R&D units. One senior leader confided to me that short of ethics violations, the company rarely terminated anyone in R&D for subpar performance. When I asked why, he said, "Our culture is like a family. Firing people is not something we're comfortable with."

The truth is that a tolerance for failure requires having extremely competent people. Attempts to create novel technological or business models are fraught with uncertainty. You often don't know what you don't know, and you have to learn as you go. "Failures" under these circumstances provide valuable lessons about paths forward. But failure can also result from poorly thought-out designs, flawed analyses, lack of transparency, and bad management. Google can encourage risk taking and failure because it can be confident that most Google employees are very competent.

Creating a culture that simultaneously values learning through failure and outstanding performance is difficult in organizations with a history of neither. A good start is for senior leadership to articulate clearly the difference between productive and unproductive failures: Productive failures yield valuable information relative to their cost. A failure should be celebrated only if it results in learning. (The cliché "celebrating failure" misses the point—we should be celebrating learning, not failure.) A simple prototype that fails to perform as expected because of a previously unknown technical issue is a failure worth celebrating if that new knowledge can be applied to future designs. Launching a badly engineered product after spending $500 million developing it is just an expensive flop.

Building a culture of competence requires clearly articulating expected standards of performance. If such standards are not well understood, difficult personnel decisions can seem capricious or, worse, be misconstrued as punishment for a failure. Senior leaders and managers throughout the organization should communicate expectations clearly and regularly. Hiring standards may need to be raised, even if that temporarily slows the growth of the company.

Managers are especially uncomfortable about firing or moving people when their "incompetence" is no fault of their own. Shifting technologies or business models can render a person who's very competent in one context incompetent in another. Consider how digitization has impacted the value of different skills in many industries. That sales representative whose deft interpersonal skills made him a superstar may no longer be as valuable to the organization as the introverted software engineer who develops the algorithms used to predict which customers are most likely to buy the company's products. In some cases, people can be retrained to develop new competences. But that's not always possible when really specialized skills (say, a PhD in applied math) are needed to do a job. Keeping people who have been rendered obsolete may be compassionate, but it's dangerous for the organization.

Maintaining a healthy balance between tolerating productive failures and rooting out incompetence is not easy. A 2015 *New York Times* article about Amazon illustrates the difficulty. The piece, which was based on interviews with more than 100 current and former employees, labeled Amazon's culture as "bruising" and recounted stories of employees crying at their desks amid enormous performance pressures. One reason striking a balance is so hard is that the causes of failure are not always clear. Did a product design turn out to be flawed because of an engineer's bad judgment or because it encountered a problem that even the most talented engineer would have missed? And in the event of bad technical or business judgments, what are the appropriate consequences? Everyone makes mistakes, but at what point does forgiveness slide into permissiveness? And at what point does setting high performance standards devolve into being cruel or failing to treat employees—regardless of their performance—with respect and dignity?

2. Willingness to Experiment but Highly Disciplined

Organizations that embrace experimentation are comfortable with uncertainty and ambiguity. They do not pretend to know all the answers up front or to be able to analyze their way to insight. They experiment to learn rather than to produce an immediately marketable product or service.

A willingness to experiment, though, does not mean working like some third-rate abstract painter who randomly throws paint at a canvas. Without discipline, almost anything can be justified as an experiment. Discipline-oriented cultures select experiments carefully on the basis of their potential learning value, and they design them rigorously to yield as much information as possible relative to the costs. They establish clear criteria at the outset for deciding whether to move forward with, modify, or kill an idea. And they face the facts generated by experiments. This may mean admitting that an initial hypothesis was wrong and that a project that once seemed promising must be killed or significantly redirected. Being more disciplined about killing losing projects makes it less risky to try new things.

A good example of a culture that combines a willingness to experiment with strict discipline is Flagship Pioneering, a Cambridge, Massachusetts, company whose business model is creating new ventures based on pioneering science. Flagship generally does not solicit business plans from independent entrepreneurs but instead uses internal teams of scientists to discover new-venture opportunities. The company has a formal exploration process whereby small teams of scientists, under the direction of one of the company's partners, undertake research on a problem of major social or economic importance—nutrition, for example. During these explorations, teams read the literature on the topic and engage the company's broad network of external scientific advisers to conceive new scientific insights. Explorations are initially unconstrained. All ideas—however seemingly unreasonable or far-fetched—are entertained. According to founder and CEO Noubar Afeyan, "Early in our explorations, we don't ask, 'Is this true?' or 'Is there data to support this idea?' We do not look for academic papers that provide proof that something is true. Instead, we ask ourselves, 'What if this were true?' or 'If only this were true, would it be valuable?'" Out of this process, teams are expected to formulate testable venture hypotheses.

Experimentation is central to Flagship's exploration process because it is how ideas are culled, reformulated, and evolved. But experimentation at Flagship differs in fundamental ways from what I often see at other companies. First, Flagship does not run experiments to validate initial ideas. Instead, teams are expected to design "killer experiments" that maximize the probability of exposing an idea's flaws. Second, unlike many established companies that heavily fund new ventures in the mistaken belief that more resources translate into more speed and more creativity, Flagship normally designs its killer experiments to cost less than $1 million and take less than six months. Such a lean approach to testing not only enables the firm to cycle through more ideas more quickly; it also makes it psychologically easier to walk away from projects that are going nowhere. It forces teams to focus narrowly on the most critical technical uncertainties and gives them faster feedback. The philosophy is to learn what you have gotten wrong early and then move quickly in more-promising directions.

Third, experimental data at Flagship is sacred. If an experiment yields negative data about a hypothesis, teams are expected to either kill or reformulate their ideas accordingly. In many organizations, getting an unexpected result is "bad news." Teams often feel the need to spin the data—describing the result as an aberration of some sort—to keep their programs alive. At Flagship, ignoring experimental data is unacceptable.

Finally, Flagship's venture team members themselves have a strong incentive to be disciplined about their programs. They gain no financial benefit from sticking with a loser program. In fact, just the opposite is true. Continuing to pursue a failed program means forgoing the opportunity to join a winning one. Again, compare this model with what is common in many companies: Having your program canceled is terrible news for you personally. It could mean loss of status or perhaps even your job. Keeping your program alive is good for your career. At Flagship, starting a successful venture, not keeping your program alive, is good for your career. (Disclosure: I serve on the board of a Flagship company, but the information in this example comes from a Harvard Business School case I researched and coauthored.)

Disciplined experimentation is a balancing act. As a leader, you want to encourage people to entertain "unreasonable ideas" and give them time to formulate their hypotheses. Demanding data to confirm or kill a hypothesis too quickly can squash the intellectual play that is necessary for creativity. Of course, not even the best-designed and well-executed experiments always yield black-and-white results. Scientific and business judgments are required to figure out which ideas to move forward, which to reformulate, and which to kill. But senior leaders need to model discipline by, for example, terminating projects they personally championed or demonstrating a willingness to change their minds in the face of the data from an experiment.

3. Psychologically Safe but Brutally Candid

Psychological safety is an organizational climate in which individuals feel they can speak truthfully and openly about problems without fear of reprisal. Decades of research on this concept by Harvard Business School professor Amy Edmondson indicate that psychologically safe environments not only help organizations avoid catastrophic errors but also support learning and innovation. For instance, when Edmondson, health care expert Richard Bohmer, and I conducted research on the adoption of a novel minimally invasive surgical technology by cardiac surgical teams, we found that teams with nurses who felt safe speaking up about problems mastered the new technology faster. If people are afraid to criticize, openly challenge superiors' views, debate the ideas of others, and raise counterperspectives, innovation can be crushed.

We all love the freedom to speak our minds without fear—we all want to be heard—but psychological safety is a two-way street. If it is safe for me to criticize your ideas, it must also be safe for you to criticize mine—whether you're higher or lower in the organization than I am. Unvarnished candor is critical to innovation because it is the means by which ideas evolve and improve. Having observed or participated in numerous R&D project team meetings, project review sessions, and board of directors meetings, I can attest that comfort with candor varies dramatically. In some organizations, people are very comfortable confronting one another about their ideas, methods, and results. Criticism is sharp. People are expected to be able to defend their proposals with data or logic.

In other places, the climate is more polite. Disagreements are restrained. Words are carefully parsed. Critiques are muffled (at least in the open). To challenge too strongly is to risk looking like you're not a team player. One manager at a large company where I worked as a consultant captured the essence of the culture when she said, "Our problem is that we are an incredibly nice organization."

When it comes to innovation, the candid organization will outperform the nice one every time. The latter confuses politeness and niceness with respect. There is nothing inconsistent about being frank and respectful. In fact, I would argue that providing and accepting frank criticism is one of the hallmarks of respect. Accepting a devastating critique of your idea is possible only if you respect the opinion of the person providing that feedback.

Still, that important caveat aside, "brutally honest" organizations are not necessarily the most comfortable environments in which to work. To outsiders and newcomers, the people may appear aggressive or hard-edged. No one minces words about design philosophies, strategy, assumptions, or perceptions of the market. Everything anyone says is scrutinized (regardless of the person's title).

Building a culture of candid debate is challenging in organizations where people tend to shy away from confrontation or where such debate is viewed as violating norms of civility. Senior leaders need to set the tone through their own behavior. They must be willing (and able) to constructively critique others' ideas without being abrasive. One way to encourage this type of culture is for them to demand criticism of their own ideas and proposals. A good blueprint for this can be found in General Dwight D. Eisenhower's battle-plan briefing to top officers of the Allied forces three weeks before the invasion of Normandy. As recounted in *Eisenhower*, a biography by Geoffrey Perret, the general started the meeting by saying, "I consider it the duty of anyone who sees a flaw in this plan not to hesitate to say so. I have no sympathy with anyone, whatever his station, who will not brook criticism. We are here to get the best possible results."

Eisenhower was not just inviting criticism or asking for input. He was literally demanding it and invoking another sacred aspect of military culture: duty. How often do you demand criticism of your ideas from your direct reports?

4. Collaboration but with Individual Accountability

Well-functioning innovation systems need information, input, and significant integration of effort from a diverse array of contributors. People who work in a collaborative culture view seeking help from colleagues as natural, regardless of whether providing such help is within their colleagues' formal job descriptions. They have a sense of collective responsibility.

But too often, collaboration gets confused with consensus. And consensus is poison for rapid decision making and navigating the complex problems associated with transformational innovation. Ultimately, someone has to make a decision and be accountable for it. An accountability culture is one where individuals are expected to make decisions and own the consequences.

There is nothing inherently inconsistent about a culture that is both collaborative and accountability-focused. Committees might review decisions or teams might provide input, but at the end of the day, specific individuals are charged with making critical design choices—deciding which features go and stay, which suppliers to use, which channel strategy makes most sense, which marketing plan is best, and so on. Pixar has created several ways to provide feedback to its movie directors, but as Ed Catmull, its cofounder and president, describes in his book *Creativity, Inc.*, the director chooses which feedback to take and which to ignore and is held accountable for the contents of the movie.

Accountability and collaboration can be complementary, and accountability can drive collaboration. Consider an organization where you personally will be held accountable for specific decisions. There is no hiding. You own the decisions you make, for better or worse. The last thing you would do is shut yourself off from feedback or from enlisting the cooperation and collaboration of people inside and outside the organization who can help you.

A good example of how accountability can drive collaborative behavior is Amazon. In researching a case for Harvard Business School, I learned that when Andy Jassy became head of Amazon's then-fledgling cloud computer business, in 2003, his biggest challenge was figuring out what services to build (hardly an easy task given that cloud services were a completely new space for Amazon—and the world). Jassy immediately sought help from Amazon's technology teams, its business and technical leaders, and external developers. Their feedback about requirements, problems, and needs was critical to the early success of what eventually became Amazon Web Services—today a profitable $12 billion business run by Jassy. For Jassy, collaboration was essential to the success of a program for which he was personally accountable.

Leaders can encourage accountability by publicly holding themselves accountable, even when that creates personal risks. Some years ago, when Paul Stoffels headed R&D at Johnson & Johnson's pharmaceutical division, his group experienced a failure in a major late-stage clinical program. (Disclosure: I have consulted for various divisions of Johnson & Johnson.) As Stoffels recounted at a meeting of J&J managers that I attended, senior leadership and the board demanded to know who was at fault when the program had its setback. "I am accountable," Stoffels replied. "If I let this go beyond me, and I point to people who took the risk to start and manage the program, then we create a risk-averse organization and are worse off. This stops with me." Stoffels, now chief scientific officer for J&J, shares this story frequently with employees throughout the corporation. He finishes with a simple promise: "You take the risk; I will take the blame." And then he urges his audience to cascade this principle down the organization.

5. Flat but Strong Leadership

An organizational chart gives you a pretty good idea of the structural flatness of a company but reveals little about its cultural flatness—how people behave and interact regardless of official position. In culturally flat organizations, people are given wide latitude to take actions, make decisions, and voice their opinions. Deference is granted on the basis of competence, not title. Culturally flat organizations can typically respond more quickly to rapidly changing circumstances because decision making is decentralized and closer to the sources of relevant information. They tend to generate a richer diversity of ideas than hierarchical ones, because they tap the knowledge, expertise, and perspectives of a broader community of contributors.

Lack of hierarchy, though, does not mean lack of leadership. Paradoxically, flat organizations require stronger leadership than hierarchical ones. Flat organizations often devolve into chaos when leadership fails to set clear strategic priorities and directions. Amazon and Google are very flat organizations in which decision making and accountability are pushed down and employees at all levels enjoy a high degree of autonomy to pursue innovative ideas. Yet both companies have incredibly strong and visionary leaders who communicate goals and articulate key principles about how their respective organizations should operate.

Here again, the balance between flatness and strong leadership requires a deft hand by management. Flatness does not mean that senior leaders distance themselves from operational details or projects. In fact, flatness allows leaders to be closer to the action. The late Sergio Marchionne, who led the resurrection of first Fiat and then Chrysler (and was the architect of their merger), commented to me during an interview for a Harvard Business School case I wrote: "At both companies, I used the same core principles for the turnaround. First, I flattened the organization. I had to reduce the distance between me and the people making decisions. [At one point, Marchionne had 46 direct reports between the two organizations.] If there is a problem, I want to know directly from the person involved, not their boss."

At both Fiat and Chrysler, Marchionne moved his office to the engineering floor so that he could be closer to product planning and development programs. He was famous both for being detail oriented and for pushing decision making down to lower levels in the organization. (With so many direct reports, it was nearly impossible for him not to!)

Getting the balance right between flatness and strong leadership is hard on top management and on employees throughout the organization. For senior leaders, it requires the capacity to articulate compelling visions and strategies (big-picture stuff) while simultaneously being adept and competent with technical and operational issues. Steve Jobs was a great example of a leader with this capacity. He laid out strong visions for Apple while being maniacally focused on technical and design issues. For employees, flatness requires them to develop their own strong leadership capacities and be comfortable with taking action and being accountable for their decisions.

Leading the Journey

All cultural changes are difficult. Organizational cultures are like social contracts specifying the rules of membership. When leaders set out to change the culture of an organization, they are in a sense breaking a social contract. It should not be surprising, then, that many people inside an organization—particularly those thriving under the existing rules—resist.

Leading the journey of building and sustaining an innovative culture is particularly difficult, for three reasons. First, because innovative cultures require a combination of seemingly contradictory behaviors, they risk creating confusion. A major project fails. Should we celebrate? Should the leader of that program be held accountable? The answer to these questions depends on the circumstances. Was the failure preventable? Were issues known in advance that could have led to different choices? Were team members transparent? Was there valuable learning from the experience? And so on. Without clarity around these nuances, people can easily get confused and even cynical about leadership's intentions.

Second, while certain behaviors required for innovative cultures are relatively easy to embrace, others will be less palatable for some in the organization. Those who think of innovation as a free-for-all will see discipline as an unnecessary constraint on their creativity; those who take comfort in the anonymity of consensus won't welcome a shift toward personal accountability. Some people will adapt readily to the new rules—a few may even surprise you—but others will not thrive.

Third, because innovative cultures are systems of interdependent behaviors, they cannot be implemented in a piecemeal fashion. Think about how the behaviors complement and reinforce one another. Highly competent people will be more comfortable with decision making and accountability—and their "failures" are likely to yield learning rather than waste. Disciplined experimentation will cost less and yield more useful information—so, again, tolerance for failed experiments becomes prudent rather than shortsighted. Accountability makes it much easier to be flat—and flat organizations create a rapid flow of information, which leads to faster, smarter decision making.

Beyond the usual things that leaders can do to drive cultural change (articulate and communicate values, model target behaviors, and so on), building an innovative culture requires some specific actions. First, leaders must be very transparent with the organization about the harder realities of innovative cultures. These cultures are not all fun and games. Many people will be excited about the prospects of having more freedom to experiment, fail, collaborate, speak up, and make decisions. But they also have to recognize that with these freedoms come some tough responsibilities. It's better to be up-front from the outset than to risk fomenting cynicism later when the rules appear to change midstream.

Second, leaders must recognize that there are no shortcuts in building an innovative culture. Too many leaders think that by breaking the organization into smaller units or creating autonomous "skunk works" they can emulate an innovative start-up culture. This approach rarely works. It confuses scale with culture. Simply breaking a big bureaucratic organization into smaller units does not magically endow them with entrepreneurial spirit. Without strong management efforts to shape values, norms, and behaviors, these offspring units tend to inherit the culture of the parent organization that spawned them. This does not mean that autonomous units or teams can't be used to experiment with a culture or to incubate a new one. They can. But the challenge of building innovative cultures inside these units should not be underestimated. And they will not be for everyone, so you will need to select very carefully who from the parent organization joins them.

Finally, because innovative cultures can be unstable, and tension between the counterbalancing forces can easily be thrown out of whack, leaders need to be vigilant for signs of excess in any area and intervene to restore balance when necessary. Unbridled, a tolerance for failure can encourage slack thinking and excuse making, but too much intolerance for incompetence can create fear of risk taking. Neither of these extremes is helpful. If taken too far, a willingness to experiment can become permission to take poorly conceived risks, and overly strict discipline can squash good but ill-formed ideas. Collaboration taken too far can bog down decision making, but excessive emphasis on individual accountability can lead to a dysfunctional climate in which everyone jealously protects his or her own interests. There is a difference between being candid and just plain nasty. Leaders need to be on the lookout for excessive tendencies, particularly in themselves. If you want your organization to strike the delicate balance required, then you as a leader must demonstrate the ability to strike that balance yourself.

Originally published in January–February 2019. Reprint R1901C

Creating a Trans-Inclusive Workplace

by Christian N. Thoroughgood, Katina B. Sawyer, and Jennica R. Webster

FOR MOST OF US, work is stressful in and of itself. Imagine carrying the added emotional weight of having to deny and suppress one of the most fundamental aspects of who you are—your gender identity—because it doesn't conform with society's norms regarding gender expression. And imagine how it would feel if you revealed your authentic self to those you work with and see every day, only to have them reject, ostracize, or ignore you as a result. (Maybe you do not have to imagine at all.)

These issues are pervasive for many trans people, who often experience stigma and discrimination, hostility, and pressure to "manage" their identities in social settings—including the workplace—to suit the expectations of others. Such experiences can set in motion a host of psychological responses that have devastating consequences for trans individuals' emotional well-being, job satisfaction, and inclination to remain with an employer.

Despite a growing global awareness of the struggles trans people face, many employers remain ill-equipped to create the policies and workplace cultures that would support trans employees. Part of the problem is a lack of knowledge about these challenges. Indeed, even companies that are LGBTQ+-friendly usually focus more on the "LGB" than on the "TQ+."

The overriding reason to address this issue is that it's simply the right thing to do. Nobody who works hard and contributes to an organization's success should ever have to feel stigmatized and fearful of coming to work each day. But that's not the only reason. A failure to adopt trans-specific policies and practices can cost businesses dearly in the form of higher turnover, decreased engagement and productivity, and possible litigation. Discriminatory behavior in general also hurts the company's brand.

Fortunately, research on how employers can more effectively attract, retain, and promote the well-being and success of their trans employees is growing. Although we are not members of the trans community, we've spent the past seven years learning from a diverse population of trans people in the course of our research as organizational psychologists specializing in gender-related issues. We've interviewed and surveyed more than 1,000 trans employees from a range of industries and professions throughout North America. In this article we share their voices and experiences and outline what we've learned.

The Roots of Stigma and Discrimination

Why do trans individuals so often face stigma and discrimination? The answer resides in how people are socialized to understand and enact gender. A large body of scholarly research in social and developmental psychology has demonstrated that gendered behavior is *learned*: From a young age, boys and girls are encouraged to display stereotypically gendered behaviors and discouraged from displaying non-normative ones. Just think about the tradition of giving pink items to baby girls and blue items to baby boys. The preference for these colors has no biological roots; in fact, pink was once considered the more "masculine" color. Yet over time little boys come to prefer blue and little girls come to prefer pink; they are subtly rewarded for liking their respective colors and may even be chastised for liking the other color. Moreover, children pick up on subtle signals from their parents and important others who enforce gender stereotypes. For example, when donning female garments during dress-up, girls

Idea in Brief

The Problem

Trans people often experience stigma and discrimination, hostility, and pressure to "manage" their identities in social settings, including the workplace.

Why It Occurs

Despite a growing global awareness of these struggles, many employers remain ill- equipped to develop policies and workplace cultures that support trans employees.

What to Do

Research and interviews or surveys of more than 1,000 trans people suggest four things companies can do: adopt basic practices of trans inclusivity involving bathroom use, dress codes, and pronouns; support gender transitions; develop trans-specific diversity trainings; and utilize resiliency interventions.

might be told they look pretty, while boys might be told they look silly. Children seek to fulfill gender expectations in order to secure parental and, later, peer acceptance. As we grow up, it becomes difficult to distinguish between expressions of gender we actually prefer and those we have been socially rewarded for.

As a result of this socialization, gender norms provide perhaps the most basic organizing framework by which people define themselves and others. And because they are widely shared and deeply rooted, they are extremely difficult to change. Thus trans people face a unique quandary. For example, when a trans woman—whose sex was assigned male at birth and who knows herself to be female—adopts typically female clothing and jewelry, she breaks with expectations regarding how she should define and express her gender.

Unfortunately, such situations most often mean that trans individuals are stigmatized—that is, socially devalued—providing a basis for discrimination against them. Studies suggest that the costs of that stigma and discrimination are steep. For example, a 2015 survey of 27,715 trans individuals residing in the United States revealed that a staggering 77% of those who had held a job in the year prior took active steps to avoid mistreatment at work, such as hiding their gender identity, delaying their gender transition (or living as their true selves only after work and on weekends), refraining from asking their employers to use their correct pronouns (*he, she, they, ze*), or quitting their jobs. Sixty-seven percent reported negative outcomes such as being fired or forced to resign, not being hired, or being denied a promotion. And nearly a quarter reported other types of mistreatment based on their gender identity or expression—for example, being required to present as the sex assigned to them at birth to keep a job, having private information about their trans identity shared without permission, or being denied access to bathrooms that align with their gender identity. Such experiences may be compounded for a trans person who holds more than one stigmatized identity—for example, a black trans woman.

Research also suggests that stigma and discrimination can result in ruminative thoughts, a negative self-image, hopelessness, social isolation, and alcohol abuse or other dysfunctional coping behaviors. Such responses pave the way for even greater mental health challenges, including major depression and anxiety.

In one of our own investigations, we collected daily survey data from 105 trans employees in the United States across two workweeks. The results revealed that 47% of participants experienced at least some discriminatory behavior on a daily basis at work, such as being the target of transphobic remarks, being ignored, or being pressured to act in "traditionally gendered" ways. They reported robust increases in hypervigilance and rumination at work the day following such an experience. The extent to which they had to be "on guard" around their coworkers and try to make sense of negative events predicted their emotional exhaustion during the workday.

In another study, this one involving 165 trans employees from various industries and occupations in North America, we replicated those results and extended them to other outcomes, including diminished job satisfaction and a greater desire to quit. One trans woman, an educator, who felt deeply unsupported by the administration after she reported being harassed, told us, "Students were being removed from my class, rumors were spread about me, and it just wasn't a great place to be working anymore." Another trans woman, who worked in retail, recalled that her direct supervisor joked about trans individuals and that customers would tell her not to bring her "lifestyle" into the workplace. As a result, she said, "I'm constantly aware of who is around me at all times. And when I'm around other people, it makes me very unsettled." A trans man in the business sector echoed this intense sense of distress: "Most of my stress that comes from work is related to just anxiety and worry [about interactions with coworkers], just constantly wondering about things that have happened and what might happen."

Employers should be aware of the business costs of ignoring these issues. A March 2012 report by the Center for American Progress indicated that companies in the United States lose an estimated $64 billion annually as a result of having to replace employees who departed because of unfairness and discrimination; many of those individuals were members of the LGBTQ+ community.

Hostility and discrimination also increase absenteeism, undermine commitment and motivation, and decrease productivity. A recent study by the Human Rights Campaign found that employee engagement declines by as much as 30% in unfriendly work environments. Although the study focused on LGBTQ+ employees more broadly, its findings are no doubt representative of trans people's experiences. In addition to hiding who they are at work, which LGB individuals often must do with respect to their sexual identity, trans people must hide their gender expression, including how they dress, speak, and present themselves.

Discriminatory workplaces also prevent companies from attracting and retaining top talent. When employers, whether knowingly or unknowingly, fail to address prejudicial behavior, they send a potent message about their indifference and develop an external reputation for being an unwelcoming place to work. (According to the Level Playing Field Institute, one in four people who experience unfairness in the workplace report being highly unlikely to recommend their organization to others.) Furthermore, laws relating to gender identity and expression, although still severely lacking in the aggregate, are evolving at the local, state, and federal levels—creating greater obligations for employers. Without comprehensive strategies for addressing issues around gender identity and expression, organizations risk being sued. Those legal actions can be expensive to litigate, distracting to business activities, and damaging to a company's reputation, in addition to involving costly payouts. But it is our hope that companies will approach trans inclusivity from a moral and ethical standpoint rather than a purely economic one.

Supporting Your Trans Workforce

Organizations should not wait for the courts to determine that trans individuals are fully protected under the law. (See the sidebar "Gender Expression and Employment Law.") Instead they should proactively incorporate gender-identity-specific nondiscrimination policies and practices throughout their businesses. That involves two key issues: protecting and promoting the rights of people of all gender identities and expressions, and increasing employees' understanding and acceptance of their trans colleagues. In a meta-analysis we conducted with Cheryl Maranto and Gary Adams, we found strong links between the degree to which employers enact these practices and the job attitudes, psychological well-being, and disclosure decisions of LGBTQ+ community members. In another study, focused specifically on trans employees, Enrica Ruggs and her coauthors found that the presence of trans-supportive policies was positively related to participants' openness about their identities and their decreased experiences of discrimination at work. However, such effects are likely to occur only when leaders model these policies consistently in both words and behavior. Also, it should be noted that effective diversity and equity practices have been found to positively impact the productivity of all employees.

Here are four practices that we recommend employers adopt. Further resources can be found through professional associations such as the Society for Human Resource Management and nonprofit organizations such as the Human Rights Campaign, Out & Equal, and the Transgender Law Center.

1. Adopt basic trans-inclusive policies

An extensive body of social psychology research suggests that human beings are highly attuned to signals regarding the value ascribed to them by others. To one degree or another, we all have a basic need to belong and a prewired, unconscious monitoring system that tracks the quality of our relationships. When we detect signs of social devaluation (apathy, disapproval, or rejection), we experience negative emotions and a loss of self-esteem. When we detect signs of social valuation (praise, affection, or admission to a desired group), just the opposite occurs. Thus inclusive policies and practices—such as those related to bathroom access, dress codes, and pronoun and name usage—send vital messages to trans employees about their value as organizational members.

Bathroom access. Instituting gender-neutral bathrooms or encouraging trans employees to use bathrooms that align with their gender identity is one important way to signal to those employees that they are valued. Diversity trainings should educate other employees on the importance of being accepting and welcoming when they find themselves in a company bathroom with a trans coworker. One of our participants, a trans man working in business, said, "When I started using the men's room at work, a number of men didn't like it. An engineer, a cisgender man in his forties who didn't work with me directly, went out of his way to make me feel safe and welcome in the men's room, and I was extremely grateful."

Some have suggested that allowing employees to use bathrooms that align with their gender identity will increase the risk of sexual harassment and assault against women. But a 2018 report published in *Sexuality Research and Social Policy* suggests that such incidents in bathrooms are rare, regardless of any gender-identity policy on bathroom usage. In fact, harassment and assault generally are most often perpetrated by straight, cisgender males against straight, cisgender females.

Dress codes. Some organizations, including Accenture, have begun to regionally implement gender-neutral dress codes. By making explicit that all employees may select from a range of options, such as dress shirts, pantsuits, and skirt suits, companies can help destigmatize varying expressions of gender. Such policies may also aid in recruitment and retention by signaling that normativity is not expected.

Pronoun and name usage. Another way to signal to trans employees that they are valued is to pay serious attention to their correct names and pronouns. Many trans people identify on the traditional binary scale—as either male or female—and thus use *he, him,* and *his* or *she, her,* and *hers* as pronouns. Yet many others who also fall under the broad category "trans"—such as genderqueer, gender-fluid, and nonbinary individuals—use alternative pronouns, such as *they, them,* and *theirs* or *ze, zir,* and *zem.*

It's clear from our conversations and research that the "misgendering" of trans employees, whether intentional or unintentional, is relatively common at work. A onetime slipup—such as using an incorrect pronoun for a colleague who has recently transitioned—may be considered an honest mistake. (One should apologize, move on, and make sure to get it right the next time.) Using the right pronouns and names on a regular basis can be more meaningful than one might think. When asked to reflect on courageous acts coworkers had performed in support of the rights of trans employees, many of our participants recalled instances in which a cisgender employee guided others on proper pronoun usage. A simple "Katie uses 'she' as a pronoun" works, as does a gentle correction: "Have you seen him?" "Yes, I saw her in the conference room."

Employers can address this issue in several ways. First, they can keep records of employees' chosen names and correct pronouns; this helps ensure that whenever possible, appropriate terms will be used for personnel and administrative purposes, such as directories, email addresses, and business cards. Second, encourage all employees to use name badges and email signatures that include their desired names and correct pronouns; this enables people to learn those names and pronouns and cultivates awareness of the varying gender identities that colleagues may possess. Third, take advantage

Gender Expression and Employment Law

LAWS REGARDING GENDER and gender expression are constantly evolving and differ according to location. In the United States no federal law prohibits discrimination against trans people, and only 19 states have explicit protections for trans workers. Additionally, the Religious Freedom Restoration Act of 1993 makes it more difficult for trans employees to file discrimination complaints against employers who justify their practices on religious grounds. Using religious freedom as a rationale, certain states have enacted laws to revoke or prohibit equal protections for trans individuals. Although gender expression has been covered in some court cases under the broader sex-discrimination protections within Title VII of the Civil Rights Act, in the absence of a federal law it remains up to the courts to decide case outcomes according to their interpretations of prior case law. Indeed, the U.S. Supreme Court in 2019 began deliberating over whether Title VII sex protections extend to LGBTQ+ populations.

At the global level, laws regarding gender expression vary widely. Many countries, including the United Kingdom, Spain, and South Africa, have trans-specific antidiscrimination protections. However, being trans is punishable by law in countries such as Saudi Arabia, Nigeria, and Malaysia. In many other countries, as in the United States, being trans is neither punishable nor protected, leaving oft-discriminated-against trans people in a state of uncertainty regarding their status as equal citizens under the law. When doing business in a global environment, it is vital to be mindful of how protections may vary and what this may mean for the safety and well-being of trans employees. Even when operating within intolerant cultural contexts, it is important to practice inclusivity consistently.

of training programs, onboarding initiatives, and employee handbook content to make clear that proper pronoun usage is part of creating an environment in which all employees feel valued and respected. Goldman Sachs, for example, recently launched an internal campaign to make employees more aware of the importance of pronouns and to encourage them to proactively share their pronouns with colleagues.

2. Support gender transitions

Transitioning is not a single event but, rather, a *process,* which begins with a deeply personal decision that usually results from years of soul-searching. The decision to come out, or disclose, at work is also complicated. People weigh the positive consequences of doing so (freedom from living a "double life" and expression of one's true self) against the negative ones (potential rejection and career ramifications). One of our study participants, a trans woman in the transportation industry, told us, "After nearly a year of soul-searching, research, therapy, support group attendance, and deep personal reflection, I 'came out' to my supervisor as transgender. . . . I finished talking, paused, and waited for her reply. My heart was in my throat. I knew this meeting might forever change the way she thought of me, and that I could not un-say what had been said."

Then the woman recounted her boss's reaction: "After a few moments, her very first words were 'We're not just a team here, we're a family, and this is your home. You have the right to be who you are and to be treated with respect and dignity. I will do everything I can to make sure your transition is as smooth and trouble-free as it can be.' She then got busy arranging meetings with the head of the department and the head of HR."

Someone deciding to transition chooses what that process will look like and how long it will take. A transition may involve gender-confirmation surgery (not all trans people undergo medical procedures). Some gender-fluid individuals spend their lives transitioning between and within various gender expressions, as they continually reinterpret and redefine themselves. Employers must develop a comprehensive approach to managing gender transitions—one that focuses on the employee but also on cultivating a work environment conducive to the transition process.

First, helping transitioning employees who elect medical procedures to cover costs—and making sure they have access to health care benefits that are gender-identity-specific—can reduce the stress and anxiety of coming out at work. Such commitment sends a highly affirming message to trans employees about their value.

Second, it is paramount that employees be asked what they need during their transitions and how they would like the process handled. Only by listening to and collaborating with them can employers ensure that people are not inadvertently "outed" without permission or before they're ready.

Gender Identity and Expression: A Glossary

PEOPLE HAVE DIFFERING LANGUAGE to describe who they are and how they want to label their identities. The terms below are frequently used, but we acknowledge that these and other definitions are constantly evolving. Further, it's important to note that individuals know their own identity best and should always be consulted about how they'd like to be referred to. (For more, see the Human Rights Campaign's glossary of terms.)

Cisgender: A gender identity that aligns with the sex assigned at birth.

Gender expression: The ways in which people—trans or not—choose to convey their gender identity through dress, verbal communication styles, and other outward behavior.

Gender fluid: Refers to people who feel more male, more female, or some combination of the two at various times, and who therefore express their gender identity more dynamically over time.

Gender identity: How one understands one's own gender, regardless of the sex assigned at birth.

Genderqueer: A gender identity and expression that are not tied to a traditional male/female view of the gender spectrum. Those who identify as genderqueer may identify as men or women, as neither, or as some combination of the two.

Trans: An umbrella term for cases in which gender does not align with societal expectations regarding the sex assigned at birth. Some people who fall under the umbrella decide to transition; others do not, because they don't define themselves according to the traditional male-female binary or because they have a more fluid view of their identity over time.

Transgender: A gender identity that does not align with the sex assigned at birth. For example, a transgender woman is someone whose sex assigned at birth was male.

Third, if approached by an employee, an HR manager can provide information concerning where to learn more about treatment options, organizational support groups, and other available resources and can develop strategies to help the employee manage work/life issues that may arise during the process. Including direct supervisors in such meetings, if the employee feels comfortable with this, can promote empathy and aid in crafting flexible and informed plans adapted to each individual's unique needs. Google, Cigna, and Chevron have implemented such initiatives.

Fourth, and equally important, our research suggests that leaders and managers must proactively cultivate a supportive work environment. The period of transitioning is particularly sensitive; indeed, individuals may be ostracized or pressured by peers to suppress their identities during this time, increasing their susceptibility to depression, anxiety, and even suicidal thinking. Moreover, any trans person seeking surgery will be questioned by the surgical team about the existence of support networks, which are often required for someone who is seeking gender-confirming procedures. Thus having supportive policies and plans in place will remove one or more barriers to care for trans employees.

Authority figures who model trans-inclusive behaviors on a consistent basis are crucial to creating a supportive environment. Many of our participants said they would not have felt comfortable inquiring about transition benefits, much less been successful in their transitions, if senior leaders and frontline managers had not shown support, which tends to have a trickle-down effect on lower-level employees. Top leaders can do this in various ways, such as by attending or presenting at conferences about trans-specific issues, publicly championing gender-inclusive dress codes and bathroom usage initiatives, and using their correct names and gender pronouns.

Of course coworkers play a key role as well. In a recent study using interview and survey data from 389 trans employees and conducted with Larry Martinez, Enrica Ruggs, and Nicholas Smith, we found that those who were relatively far along in their transitions were more satisfied with their jobs, felt a greater sense of "fit" in their workplaces, and reported less discrimination than those who had not transitioned or were less far along in the process. We also found that this effect was explained *not* by participants' sense of consistency between their inner gender identity and their outward expression of gender—what is referred to as *action authenticity*—but, rather, by the perception that coworkers had the same understanding of their gender that the participants did, which is known as *relational authenticity*. One participant, a trans man who works as a museum curator, said, "There was a point where people started seeing me as just one of the guys. And I think that at that point I started feeling like I fit in a lot better. It's the individuals [coworkers] who make that possible." In a poignant example from a separate study, a trans woman in manufacturing reported a moment at a company function: "I appeared in a dress for the first time at a party. One of the housekeeping aides grabbed my hand and pulled me onto the dance floor in front of everyone. His courage in accepting who I was in front of all our coworkers can bring me to tears to this day."

To help in cultivating supportive relationships, work groups should be told when those who are transitioning will be out of the office, whether they will return part-time, and what work will have to be covered during their absence. Emphasizing the need for coworkers to show sensitivity, provide emotional support, and act in ways that affirm the gender identity of their colleagues is crucial. For example, people can make it clear that they are available to talk about any issues related to transitioning or gender expression—while following trans employees' lead about when and where to have those conversations. That approach enhances feelings of support and care and allows trans employees to be comfortable having honest conversations with their colleagues. Even well-intentioned employees may be nervous about their ability to support a colleague through a transition, and employers can help ease some of their anxiety by taking the above steps.

3. Develop trans-specific diversity training

More general training on gender-identity topics is also essential. Although media coverage has helped facilitate conversations about gender identity and expression, corporate diversity trainings still have room for improvement. We offer two recommendations:

1. **Include contact with those who identify along the trans identity spectrum.** A large body of research on the "contact hypothesis" suggests that providing opportunities to build relationships with specific groups—to hear their stories, appreciate their challenges,

and gain empathy—is critical for shifting attitudes and behavior toward them. However, it is not the responsibility of members of the LGBTQ+ community to educate others or to be visible in this way; "out" trans employees should be included in trainings only if they are willing. If they're not, many corporate training firms and LGBTQ+ nonprofit organizations offer training of this nature.

2. Help cisgender employees develop the skills to become informal champions of their transgender colleagues. Research suggests that many people lack the knowledge and confidence to challenge prejudice. That's why some companies have sought to equip their employees, especially leaders, with concrete strategies for stepping out of their comfort zones and engaging in "courageous conversations" regarding difficult diversity-related topics. For example, an employee who witnesses biased behavior is encouraged to respectfully but directly call it out. That might mean pulling someone aside to explain the potential damage from a biased comment, or having coffee with someone to tactfully share why a behavior was noninclusive. The chairman of PwC launched the CEO Action for Diversity & Inclusion coalition to normalize diversity-related conversations across top-level leaders in large companies. At Bank of America employees are encouraged to discuss gender, race, and other identity-related issues in a respectful, learning-focused manner.

These efforts pay off. In a forthcoming study we will report that cisgender employees who challenge noninclusive policies and behavior send an important message of inclusion to their trans colleagues. Our findings suggest that these behaviors may come in three related forms: *advocacy,* such as taking the initiative to publicly support trans causes; *defending,* such as protecting trans coworkers from judgment or hostility; and *educating,* such as spreading awareness of trans issues in the organization. We found that trans individuals who had recently witnessed these behaviors tended to report an increased sense of worth as organizational members, were more satisfied with their jobs, and were less emotionally depleted by work.

One trans man in government recalled feeling immense gratitude toward his assistant when she spoke out after he was treated poorly by a manager. "This came about as I sat at a lunch table at an empty chair," he recalled. "When he saw I was sitting there, [he] jumped up like he had sat next to a very large spider. She [my assistant] voiced, 'Scott, that was so rude'—twice! That brought me to an island of relief." Courageous acts like this predicted individuals' job satisfaction and well-being a full six weeks later.

Despite the good intentions of many cisgender employees, however, trans people may not always want others to represent their interests, especially when those others lack in-depth knowledge of the various issues, challenges, and nuances surrounding their work and life experiences. And research suggests that employees who possess a "savior mentality" (that is, are motivated by a desire to be perceived as good people) may end up doing more harm than good. Accordingly, HR practitioners should train employees to appropriately ask whether trans colleagues prefer to speak up for themselves. (If they wish to be, trans employees should be involved in this training.) The simple act of consulting before taking action gives a trans person agency and autonomy in deciding how the situation should be handled.

4. Utilize interventions to build resiliency
Research also supports the idea that trans individuals can benefit from interventions to help them manage their stress. In a recent two-week experience sampling study of ours, we found evidence to suggest that mindfulness—a state of nonjudgmental attention to present-moment experiences—can insulate trans employees from emotional exhaustion the day after experiencing a stigmatizing event at work. This effect was explained by a reduction in defensive, distrustful patterns of thinking such as hypervigilance and rumination.

Unfortunately, it's not realistic to assume that prejudice toward trans employees will be eliminated quickly and easily through workplace initiatives. Such changes take time. And although the main goal of employers should be to root out prejudice at a structural level through formal diversity policies and practices, it's also important to offer tools—such as mindfulness training, cognitive behavioral training, and self-compassion training—for reducing the harmful outcomes that stigma creates in marginalized populations.

Only when people feel totally authentic and connected with their organizations can they achieve their full potential at work. Trans employees are no exception. Yet few companies have succeeded in creating an inclusive work environment for people who don't identify with societal gender norms. We hope that the research and the proactive steps we've outlined will help change that. Employers that get this right aren't just being savvy from a business standpoint. They are also crafting a corporate legacy—one in which human dignity is prioritized and doing the right thing by employees is regarded as fundamental to success.

Originally published in March–April 2020. Reprint R2002J

When Data Creates Competitive Advantage

... and When It Doesn't

by Andrei Hagiu and Julian Wright

MANY EXECUTIVES AND INVESTORS ASSUME that it's possible to use customer-data capabilities to gain an unbeatable competitive edge. The more customers you have, the more data you can gather, and that data, when analyzed with machine-learning tools, allows you to offer a better product that attracts more customers. You can then collect even more data and eventually marginalize your competitors in the same way that businesses with sizable network effects do. Or so the thinking goes. More often than not, this assumption is wrong. In most instances people grossly overestimate the advantage that data confers.

The virtuous cycles generated by data-enabled learning may look similar to those of regular network effects, wherein an offering—like a social media platform—becomes more valuable as more people use it and ultimately garners a critical mass of users that shuts out competitors. But in practice regular network effects last longer and tend to be more powerful. To establish the strongest competitive position, you need them *and* data-enabled learning. However, few companies are able to develop both. Nevertheless under the right conditions customer-generated data can help you build competitive defenses, even if network effects aren't present. In this article we'll walk you through what those conditions are and explain how to evaluate whether they apply to your business.

What Has Changed?

Companies built on data have been around for a long time. Take credit bureaus and the information aggregators LexisNexis, Thomson Reuters, and Bloomberg, just to name a few. Those companies are protected by significant barriers to entry because of the economies of scale involved in acquiring and structuring huge amounts of data, but their business models don't involve gleaning data from customers and mining it to understand how to improve offerings.

Gathering customer information and using it to make better products and services is an age-old strategy, but the process used to be slow, limited in scope, and difficult to scale up. For automakers, consumer-packaged-goods companies, and many other traditional manufacturers, it required crunching sales data, conducting customer surveys, and holding focus groups. But the sales data often wasn't linked to individual customers, and since surveys and focus groups were expensive and time-consuming, only data from a relatively small number of customers was collected.

That changed dramatically with the advent of the cloud and new technologies that allow firms to quickly process and make sense of vast amounts of data. Internet-connected products and services can now directly collect information on customers, including their personal details, search behavior, choices of content, communications, social media posts, GPS location, and usage patterns. After machine-learning algorithms analyze this "digital exhaust," a company's offerings can be automatically adjusted to reflect the findings and even tailored to individuals.

These developments make data-enabled learning much more powerful than the customer insights companies produced in the past. They do not, however, guarantee defensible barriers.

Idea in Brief

The Assumption

Companies can build winner-take-all positions by collecting and analyzing customer data. The more customers a firm has, the more data it can gather and mine; the resulting insights allow it to offer a better product that attracts even more customers, from which it can collect still more data.

The Reality

Even when customer data does confer a competitive advantage, it gives rise to network effects only infrequently. And that advantage may not last.

The Solution

To understand the edge that data-enabled learning can provide, companies should answer seven questions, which examine the value of the data; whether its marginal value drops quickly; how fast it becomes obsolete; whether it's proprietary; whether the improvements from it can be easily imitated; whether they enhance the product for current users, other users, or both; and how fast insights can be incorporated into products.

Building Moats with Data-Enabled Learning

To determine to what degree a competitive advantage provided by data-enabled learning is sustainable, companies should answer seven questions:

1. How much value is added by customer data relative to the stand-alone value of the offering?

The higher the value added, the greater the chance that it will create a lasting edge. Let's look at a business where the value of customer data is very high: Mobileye, the leading provider of advanced driver-assistance systems (ADAS), which include collision-prevention and lane-departure warnings for vehicles. Mobileye sells its systems mainly to car manufacturers, which test them extensively before incorporating them into their products. It's crucial for the systems to be fail-safe, and the testing data is essential to improving their accuracy. By gathering it from dozens of its customers, Mobileye has been able to raise the accuracy of its ADAS to 99.99%.

Conversely, the value of learning from customers is relatively low for makers of smart televisions. Some now include software that can provide personalized recommendations for shows or movies based on an individual's viewing habits as well as what's popular with other users. So far, consumers don't care much about this feature (which is also offered by streaming service providers such as Amazon and Netflix). They largely consider TV size, picture quality, ease of use, and durability when making purchasing decisions. If learning from customers was a bigger factor, perhaps the smart TV business would be less competitive.

2. How quickly does the marginal value of data-enabled learning drop off?

In other words, how soon does the company reach a point where additional customer data no longer enhances the value of an offering? The more slowly the marginal value decreases, the stronger the barrier is. Note that when answering this question, you should judge the value of the learning by customers' willingness to pay and not by some other application-specific measure, such as the percentage of chat-bot queries that could be answered correctly or the fraction of times a movie recommendation was clicked on.

Let's say you graphed the accuracy of Mobileye's ADAS as a function of customer usage (total miles driven by car manufacturers testing it) and found that a few manufacturers and a moderate level of testing would be sufficient to achieve, say, 90% accuracy—but that a lot more testing with a bigger set of car manufacturers would be needed to get to 99%, let alone 99.99%. Interpreting that to mean that the customer data's marginal value was rapidly decreasing would, of course, be incorrect: The value of the additional 9-percentage-point (or even a 0.99-point) improvement in accuracy remains extremely high, given the life-or-death implications. It would be difficult for any individual car manufacturer—even the largest one—to generate the necessary amount of data on its own or for any potential Mobileye competitors to replicate the data. That's why Mobileye was able to carve out a dominant position in the ADAS market, making it a highly attractive acquisition for Intel, which bought it for $15 billion in 2017.

When the marginal value of learning from customer data remains high even after a very large customer base has been acquired, products and services tend to have significant competitive advantages. You can see this with systems designed to predict rare diseases (such as those offered by RDMD) and online search engines such as Baidu and Google. Although Microsoft has invested many years and billions of dollars in Bing, it has been unable to shake Google's dominance in search. Search engines and disease-prediction systems all need huge amounts of user data to provide consistently reliable results.

A counterexample of a business where the marginal value of user data drops off quickly is smart thermostats. These products need only a few days to learn users' temperature preferences throughout the day. In this context data-enabled learning can't provide much competitive advantage. Although it launched the first smart thermostats that learn from customer behavior in 2011, Nest (acquired by Google in 2014) now faces significant competition from players such as Ecobee and Honeywell.

3. How fast does the relevance of the user data depreciate?
If the data becomes obsolete quickly, then all other things being equal, it will be easier for a rival to enter the market, because it doesn't need to match the incumbent's years of learning from data.

All the data Mobileye has accumulated over the years from car manufacturers remains valuable in the current versions of its products. So does the data on search-engine users that Google has collected over decades. Although searches for some terms may become rare over time while searches for new ones might start appearing more frequently, having years of historical search data is of undeniable value in serving today's users. Their data's low depreciation rate helps explain why both Mobileye and Google Search have proved to be very resilient businesses.

With casual social games for computers and mobile devices, however, the value of learning from user data tends to decrease quickly. In 2009 this market took off when Zynga introduced its highly successful FarmVille game. While the company was famous for relying heavily on user-data analytics to make design decisions, it turned out that the insights learned from one game did not transfer very well to the next: Casual social games are subject to fads, and user preferences shift quickly over time, making it difficult to build sustainable data-driven competitive advantages. After a few more successes, including FarmVille 2 and CityVille, Zynga stopped producing new hits, and in 2013 it lost nearly half its user base. It was superseded by game makers like Supercell (Clash of Clans) and Epic Games (Fortnite). After reaching a peak of $10.4 billion in 2012, Zynga's market value languished below $4 billion for most of the next six years.

4. Is the data proprietary—meaning it can't be purchased from other sources, easily copied, or reverse-engineered?

Having unique customer data with few or no substitutes is critical to creating a defensible barrier. Consider Adaviv, a Boston-area start-up we've invested in, which offers a crop-management system that allows growers (now primarily of cannabis) to continuously monitor individual plants. The system relies on AI, computer-vision software, and a proprietary data-annotation technique to track plant biometrics not visible to the human eye, such as early signs of disease or lack of adequate nutrients. It then translates the data into insights that growers can use to prevent disease outbreaks and improve yields. The more growers Adaviv serves, the broader the range of variants, agricultural conditions, and other factors it can learn about, and the greater the accuracy of its predictions for new and existing customers. Contrast its situation with that of spam-filter providers, which can acquire user data relatively cheaply. That helps explain the existence of dozens of such providers.

It's important to keep in mind that technological progress can undermine a position based on unique or proprietary data. A case in point is speech-recognition software. Historically, users needed to train the software to understand their individual voices and speech patterns, and the more a person used it, the more accurate it became. This market was dominated by Nuance's Dragon solutions for many years. However, the past decade has seen rapid improvements in speaker-independent speech-recognition systems, which can be trained on publicly available sets of speech data and take minimal or no time to learn to understand a new speaker's voice. These advances have allowed many companies to provide new speech-recognition applications (automated customer service over the phone, automated meeting transcript services, virtual assistants), and they're putting increasing pressure on Nuance in its core markets.

5. How hard is it to imitate product improvements that are based on customer data?

Even when the data is unique or proprietary and produces valuable insights, it's difficult to build a durable competitive advantage if the resulting enhancements can be copied by competitors without similar data.

A couple of factors affect companies' ability to overcome this challenge. One is whether the improvements are hidden or deeply embedded in a complex production process, making them hard to replicate. Pandora, the music-streaming service, benefits from this barrier. Its offering leveraged the firm's proprietary Music Genome Project, which categorized millions of songs on the basis of some 450 attributes, allowing Pandora to customize radio stations to individual users' preferences. The more a user listens to his or her stations and rates songs up or down, the better Pandora can tailor musical selections to that user. Such customization cannot be easily imitated by any rival because it is deeply tied to the Music Genome Project. In contrast, the design improvements based on learning from the customer use of many office-productivity software products—such as Calendly for coordinating calendars and Doodle for polling people about meeting times—can be easily observed and copied. That's why dozens of companies offer similar software.

The second factor is how quickly the insights from customer data change. The more rapidly they do so, the harder they are for others to imitate. For example, many design features of the Google Maps interface can be easily copied (and they have been, by Apple Maps, among others). But a key part of Google Maps' value is its ability to predict traffic and recommend optimal routes, which is much harder to copy because it leverages real-time user data that becomes obsolete within minutes. Only companies with similarly large user bases (such as Apple in the United States) can hope to replicate that feature. Apple Maps is closing the gap with Google Maps in the United States, but not in countries where Apple has a relatively small user base.

6. Does the data from one user help improve the product for the same user or for others?

Ideally, it will do both, but the difference between the two is important. When data from one user improves the product for that person, the firm can individually customize it, creating switching costs. When data from one user improves the product for other users, this can—but may not—create network effects. Both kinds of enhancements help provide a barrier to entry, but the former makes *existing* customers very sticky, whereas the latter provides a key advantage in competing for *new* customers.

For example, Pandora was the first big player in digital music streaming but then fell behind Spotify and Apple Music, which are still growing. As we noted, Pandora's main selling point is that it can tailor stations to each user's tastes. But learning across users is very limited: An individual user's up-or-down votes allow Pandora to identify music attributes that the user likes and then serve that person songs sharing those attributes. In contrast, Spotify focused a lot more on providing users with sharing and discovery features, such as the ability to search and listen to other people's stations, thereby creating direct network effects and luring additional customers. Pandora's service remains available only in the United States (where it has a base of loyal users), while Spotify and Apple Music have become global players. And though Pandora was acquired by Sirius XM for $3.5 billion in February 2019, Spotify became a public company in April 2018 and as of early November 2019 was worth $26 billion. Clearly, customization based on learning from an individual user's data helps keep existing customers locked in, but it doesn't lead to the type of exponential growth that network effects produce.

7. How fast can the insights from user data be incorporated into products?

Rapid learning cycles make it hard for competitors to catch up, especially if multiple product-improvement cycles occur during the average customer's contract. But when it takes years or successive product generations to make enhancements based on the data, competitors have more of a chance to innovate in the interim and start collecting their own user data. So the competitive advantage from customer data is stronger when the learning from *today's* customers translates into more-frequent improvements of the product for those same customers rather than just for *future* customers of the product or service. Several of the product examples we've discussed already—maps, search engines, and AI-based crop-management systems—can be quickly updated to incorporate the learning from current customers.

A counterexample is offered by direct online lenders, such as LendUp and LendingPoint, which learn how to make better loan decisions by examining users' repayment history and how it correlates with various aspects of users' profiles and behavior. Here, the only learning that is relevant to *current* borrowers is that from *previous* borrowers, which is already reflected in the contracts and rates that current borrowers are offered. There's no reason for borrowers to care about any future learning that the lender may benefit from, since their existing contracts won't be affected. For that reason, customers don't worry about how many other borrowers will sign up when deciding whether to take a loan from a particular lender. Existing borrowers might prefer to stick with their current lenders, which know them better than other lenders do, but the market for new borrowers remains very competitive.

Does Data Confer Network Effects?

The answers to questions 6 and 7 will tell you whether data-enabled learning will create true network effects. When learning from one customer translates into a better experience for other customers *and* when that learning can be incorporated into a product fast enough to benefit its current users, customers will care about how many other people are adopting the product. The mechanism at work here is very similar to the one underlying network effects with online platforms. The difference is that platform users prefer to join bigger networks because they want more people to interact with, not because more users generate more insights that improve products.

Let's look at Google Maps again. Drivers use it in part because they expect many others to employ it too, and the more traffic data the software gathers from them, the better its predictions on road conditions and travel times. Google Search and Adaviv's AI-based crop-management system also enjoy data-enabled network effects.

Like regular network effects, data-enabled ones can create barriers to entry. Both types of effects present a huge cold-start, or chicken-or-egg, challenge: Businesses aiming to build regular network effects need to attract some minimum number of users to get the effects started, and those aiming to achieve data-enabled network effects need some initial amount of data to start the virtuous cycle of learning.

Despite these similarities, regular network effects and data-enabled network effects have key differences, and they tend to make advantages based on the regular ones stronger. First, the cold-start problem is usually less severe with data-enabled network effects, because buying data is easier than buying customers. Often, alternative sources of data, even if not perfect, can significantly level the playing field by removing the need for a big customer base.

Second, to produce lasting data-enabled network effects, the firm has to work constantly to learn from customer data. In contrast, as Intuit cofounder Scott Cook has often said, "products that benefit from [regular] network effects get better while I sleep." With regular network effects, interactions between customers (and possibly with third-party providers of complementary offerings) create value even if the platform stops innovating. Even if a new social network offered users objectively better features than Facebook does (for instance, better privacy protection), it would still have to contend with Facebook's powerful network effects—users want to be on the same social platform as most other users.

Third, in many cases nearly all the benefits of learning from customer data can be achieved with relatively low numbers of customers. And in some applications (like speech recognition), dramatic improvements in AI will reduce the need for customer data to the point where the value of data-enabled learning might disappear completely. Regular network effects, on the other hand, extend further and are more resilient: An additional customer still typically enhances value for existing customers (who can interact or transact with him or her), even when the number of existing customers is already very large.

_____

As even mundane consumer products become smart and connected—new kinds of clothing, for instance, can now react to weather conditions and track mileage and vital signs—data-enabled learning will be used to enhance and personalize more and more offerings. However, their providers won't build strong competitive positions unless the value added by customer data is high and lasting, the data is proprietary and leads to product improvements that are hard to copy, or the data-enabled learning creates network effects.

In the decades ahead, improving offerings with customer data will be a prerequisite for staying in the game, and it may give incumbents an edge over new entrants. But in most cases it will not generate winner-take-all dynamics. Instead, the most valuable and powerful businesses for the foreseeable future will be those that are both built on regular network effects and enhanced by data-enabled learning, like Alibaba's and Amazon's marketplaces, Apple's App Store, and Facebook's social networks.

Originally published in January–February 2020. Reprint R2001G

Your Approach to Hiring Is All Wrong

by Peter Cappelli

BUSINESSES HAVE NEVER done as much hiring as they do today. They've never spent as much money doing it. And they've never done a worse job of it.

For most of the post–World War II era, large corporations went about hiring this way: Human resources experts prepared a detailed *job analysis* to determine what tasks the job required and what attributes a good candidate should have. Next they did a *job evaluation* to determine how the job fit into the organizational chart and how much it should pay, especially compared with other jobs. Ads were posted, and applicants applied. Then came the task of sorting through the applicants. That included skills tests, reference checks, maybe personality and IQ tests, and extensive interviews to learn more about them as people. William H. Whyte, in *The Organization Man,* described this process as going on for as long as a week before the winning candidate was offered the job. The vast majority of non-entry-level openings were filled from within.

Today's approach couldn't be more different. Census data shows, for example, that the majority of people who took a new job last year weren't searching for one: Somebody came and got them. Companies seek to fill their recruiting funnel with as many candidates as possible, especially "passive candidates," who aren't looking to move. Often employers advertise jobs that don't exist, hoping to find people who might be useful later on or in a different context.

The recruiting and hiring function has been eviscerated. Many U.S. companies—about 40%, according to research by Korn Ferry—have outsourced much if not all of the hiring process to "recruitment process outsourcers," which in turn use subcontractors, typically in India and the Philippines. The subcontractors scour LinkedIn and social media to find potential candidates. They sometimes contact them directly to see whether they can be persuaded to apply for a position and negotiate the salary they're willing to accept. (The recruiters get incentive pay if they negotiate the amount down.) To hire programmers, for example, these subcontractors can scan websites that programmers might visit, trace their "digital exhaust" from cookies and other user-tracking measures to identify who they are, and then examine their curricula vitae.

At companies that still do their own recruitment and hiring, managers trying to fill open positions are largely left to figure out what the jobs require and what the ads should say. When applications come—always electronically—applicant-tracking software sifts through them for key words that the hiring managers want to see. Then the process moves into the Wild West, where a new industry of vendors offers an astonishing array of smart-sounding tools that claim to predict who will be a good hire. They use voice recognition, body language, clues on social media, and especially machine learning algorithms—everything but tea leaves. Entire publications are devoted to what these vendors are doing.

The big problem with all these new practices is that we don't know whether they actually produce satisfactory hires. Only about a third of U.S. companies report that they monitor whether their hiring practices lead to good employees; few of them do so carefully, and only a minority even track cost per hire and time to hire. Imagine if the CEO asked how an advertising campaign had gone, and the response was "We have a good idea how long it took to roll out and what it cost, but we haven't looked to see whether we're selling more."

Hiring talent remains the number one concern of CEOs in the most recent Conference Board Annual Survey; it's also the top concern of the entire executive suite. PwC's 2017 CEO survey reports that chief executives view the unavailability of talent and skills as the biggest

Idea in Brief

The Problem

Employers continue to hire at a high rate and spend enormous sums to do it. But they don't know whether their approaches are effective at finding and selecting good candidates.

The Root Causes

Businesses focus on external candidates and don't track the results of their approaches. They often use outside vendors and high-tech tools that are unproven and have inherent flaws.

The Solution

Return to filling most positions by promoting from within. Measure the results produced by vendors and new tools, and be on the lookout for discrimination and privacy violations.

---

threat to their business. Employers also spend an enormous amount on hiring—an average of $4,129 per job in the United States, according to Society for Human Resource Management estimates, and many times that amount for managerial roles—and the United States fills a staggering 66 million jobs a year. Most of the $20 billion that companies spend on human resources vendors goes to hiring.

Why do employers spend so much on something so important while knowing so little about whether it works?

Where the Problem Starts

Survey after survey finds employers complaining about how difficult hiring is. There may be many explanations, such as their having become very picky about candidates, especially in the slack labor market of the Great Recession. But clearly they are hiring much more than at any other time in modern history, for two reasons.

The first is that openings are now filled more often by hiring from the outside than by promoting from within. In the era of lifetime employment, from the end of World War II through the 1970s, corporations filled roughly 90% of their vacancies through promotions and lateral assignments. Today the figure is a third or less. When they hire from outside, organizations don't have to pay to train and develop their employees. Since the restructuring waves of the early 1980s, it has been relatively easy to find experienced talent outside. Only 28% of talent acquisition leaders today report that internal candidates are an important source of people to fill vacancies—presumably because of less internal development and fewer clear career ladders.

Less promotion internally means that hiring efforts are no longer concentrated on entry-level jobs and recent graduates. (If you doubt this, go to the "careers" link on any company website and look for a job opening that doesn't require prior experience.) Now companies must be good at hiring across most levels, because the candidates they want are already doing the job somewhere else. These people don't need training, so they may be ready to contribute right away, but they are much harder to find.

The second reason hiring is so difficult is that retention has become tough: Companies hire from their competitors and vice versa, so they have to keep replacing people who leave. Census and Bureau of Labor Statistics data shows that 95% of hiring is done to fill existing positions. Most of those vacancies are caused by voluntary turnover. LinkedIn data indicates that the most common reason employees consider a position elsewhere is career advancement— which is surely related to employers' not promoting to fill vacancies.

The root cause of most hiring, therefore, is drastically poor retention. Here are some simple ways to fix that:

Track the percentage of openings filled from within

An adage of business is that we manage what we measure, but companies don't seem to be applying that maxim to tracking hires. Most are shocked to learn how few of their openings are filled from within—is it really the case that their people can't handle different and bigger roles?

Require that all openings be posted internally

Internal job boards were created during the dot-com boom to reduce turnover by making it easier for people to find new jobs within their existing employer. Managers weren't even allowed to know if a subordinate was looking to move within the company, for fear that they would try to block that person and he or she would leave. But during the Great Recession employees weren't quitting, and many companies slid back to the old model whereby managers could prevent their subordinates from moving internally. J.R. Keller, of Cornell University, has found that when managers could fill a vacancy with someone they already had in mind, they ended up with employees who performed more poorly than those hired when the job had been posted and anyone could apply. The commonsense explanation for this is that few enterprises really know what talent and capabilities they have.

Recognize the costs of outside hiring

In addition to the time and effort of hiring, my colleague Matthew Bidwell found, outside hires take three years to perform as well as internal hires in the same job, while internal hires take seven years to earn as much as outside hires are paid. Outside hiring also causes current employees to spend time and energy positioning themselves for jobs elsewhere. It disrupts the culture and burdens peers who must help new hires figure out how things work.

None of this is to suggest that outside hiring is necessarily a bad idea. But unless your company is a Silicon Valley gazelle, adding new jobs at a furious pace, you should ask yourself some serious questions if most of your openings are being filled from outside.

A different approach for dealing with retention (which seems creepy to some) is to try to determine who is interested in leaving and then intervene. Vendors like Jobvite comb social media and public sites for clues, such as LinkedIn profile updates. Measuring "flight risk" is one of the most common goals of companies that do their own sophisticated HR analytics. This is reminiscent of the early days of job boards, when employers would try to find out who was posting résumés and either punish them or embrace them, depending on leadership's mood.

Whether companies should be examining social media content in relation to hiring or any other employment action is a challenging ethical question. On one hand, the information is essentially public and may reveal relevant information. On the other hand, it is

Protecting Against Discrimination

FINDING OUT WHETHER YOUR PRACTICES result in good hires is not only basic to good management but the only real defense against claims of adverse impact and discrimination. Other than white males under age 40 with no disabilities or work-related health problems, workers have special protections under federal and state laws against hiring practices that may have an adverse impact on them. As a practical matter, that means if members of a particular group are less likely to be recruited or hired, the employer must show that the hiring process is not discriminatory.

The only defense against evidence of adverse impact is for the employer to show that its hiring practices are valid—that is, they predict who will be a good employee in meaningful and statistically significant ways—and that no alternative would predict as well with less adverse impact. That analysis must be conducted with data on the employer's own applicants and hires. The fact that the vendor that sold you the test you use has evidence that it was valid in other contexts is not sufficient.

---

invasive, and candidates are rarely asked for permission to scrutinize their information. Hiring a private detective to shadow a candidate would also gather public information that might be relevant, yet most people would view it as an unacceptable invasion of privacy.

The Hiring Process

When we turn to hiring itself, we find that employers are missing the forest for the trees: Obsessed with new technologies and driving down costs, they largely ignore the ultimate goal: making the best possible hires. Here's how the process should be revamped:

Don't post "phantom jobs"

It costs nothing to post job openings on a company website, which are then scooped up by Indeed and other online companies and pushed out to potential job seekers around the world. Thus it may be unsurprising that some of these jobs don't really exist. Employers may simply be fishing for candidates. ("Let's see if someone really great is out there, and if so, we'll create a position for him or her.") Often job ads stay up even after positions have been filled, to keep collecting candidates for future vacancies or just because it takes more effort to pull the ad down than to leave it up. Sometimes ads are posted by unscrupulous recruiters looking for résumés to pitch to clients elsewhere. Because these phantom jobs make the labor market look tighter than it really is, they are a problem for economic policy makers as well as for frustrated job seekers. Companies should take ads down when jobs are filled.

Design jobs with realistic requirements

Figuring out what the requirements of a job should be—and the corresponding attributes candidates must have—is a bigger challenge now, because so many companies have reduced the number of internal recruiters whose function, in part, is to push back on hiring managers' wish lists. ("That job doesn't require 10 years of experience," or "No one with all those qualifications will be willing to accept the salary you're proposing to pay.") My earlier research found that companies piled on job requirements, baked them into the applicant-tracking software that sorted résumés according to binary decisions (yes, it has the key word; no, it doesn't), and then found that virtually no applicants met all the criteria. Trimming recruiters, who have expertise in hiring, and handing the process over to hiring managers is a prime example of being penny-wise and pound-foolish.

Reconsider your focus on passive candidates

The recruiting process begins with a search for experienced people who aren't looking to move. This is based on the notion that something may be wrong with anyone who wants to leave his or her current job. (Of the more than 20,000 talent professionals who responded to a LinkedIn survey in 2015, 86% said their recruiting organizations focused "very much so" or "to some extent" on passive candidates; I suspect that if anything, that number has since grown.) Recruiters know that the vast majority of people are open to moving at the right price: Surveys of employees find that only about 15% are *not* open to moving. As the economist Harold Demsetz said when asked by a competing university if he was happy working where he was: "Make me unhappy."

Fascinating evidence from the LinkedIn survey cited above shows that although self-identified "passive" job seekers are different from "active" job seekers, it's not in the way we might think. The number one factor that would encourage the former to move is more money. For active candidates the top factor is better work and career opportunities. More active than passive job seekers report that they are passionate about their work, engaged in improving their skills, and reasonably satisfied with their current jobs. They seem interested in moving because they are ambitious, not because they want higher pay.

Employers spend a vastly disproportionate amount of their budgets on recruiters who chase passive candidates, but on average they fill only 11% of their positions with individually targeted people, according to research by Gerry Crispin and Chris Hoyt, of CareerXroads. I know of no evidence that passive candidates become better employees, let alone that the process is cost-effective. If you focus on passive candidates, think carefully about what that actually gets you. Better yet, check your data to find out.

Understand the limits of referrals

The most popular channel for finding new hires is through employee referrals; up to 48% come from them, according to LinkedIn research. It seems like a cheap way to go, but does it produce better hires? Many employers think so. It's hard to know whether that's true, however, given that they don't check. And research by Emilio Castilla and colleagues suggests otherwise: They find that when referrals work out better than other hires, it's because their referrers look after them and essentially onboard them. If a referrer leaves before the new hire begins, the latter's performance is no better than that of nonreferrals, which is why it makes sense to pay referral bonuses six months or so after the person is hired—if he or she is still there.

A downside to referrals, of course, is that they can lead to a homogeneous workforce, because the people we know tend to be like us. This matters greatly for organizations interested in diversity, since recruiting is the only avenue allowed under U.S. law to increase diversity in a workforce. The Supreme Court has ruled that demographic criteria cannot be used even to break ties among candidates.

Measure the results

Few employers know which channel produces the best candidates at the lowest cost because they don't track the outcomes. Tata is an exception: It has long done what I advocate. For college recruiting, for example, it calculates which schools send it employees who perform the best, stay the longest, and are paid the lowest starting wage. Other employers should follow suit and monitor recruiting channels and employees' performance to identify which sources produce the best results.

Persuade fewer people to apply

The hiring industry pays a great deal of attention to "the funnel," whereby readers of a company's job postings become applicants, are interviewed, and ultimately are offered jobs. Contrary to the popular belief that the U.S. job market is extremely tight right now, most jobs still get lots of applicants. Recruiting and hiring consultants and vendors estimate that about 2% of applicants receive offers. Unfortunately, the main effort to improve hiring—virtually always aimed at making it faster and cheaper—has been to shovel more applicants into the funnel. Employers do that primarily through marketing, trying to get out the word that they are great places to work. Whether doing this is a misguided way of trying to attract better hires or just meant to make the organization feel more desirable isn't clear.

Much better to go in the other direction: Create a smaller but better-qualified applicant pool to improve the yield. Here's why: Every applicant costs you money—especially now, in a labor market where applicants have started to "ghost" employers, abandoning their applications midway through the process. Every application also exposes a company to legal risk, because the company has obligations to candidates (not to discriminate, for example) just as it does to employees. And collecting lots of applicants in a wide funnel means that a great many of them won't fit the job or the company, so employers have to rely on the next step of the hiring process—selection—to weed them out. As we will see, employers aren't good at that.

The grass is always greener . . .
Organizations are much more interested in external talent than in their own employees to fill vacancies.

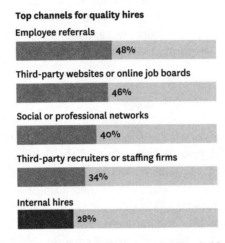

Top channels for quality hires

Employee referrals
48%

Third-party websites or online job boards
46%

Social or professional networks
40%

Third-party recruiters or staffing firms
34%

Internal hires
28%

Source: LinkedIn, based on a 2017 survey of 3,973 talent-acquisition decision makers who work in corporate HR departments and are LinkedIn members.

Once people are candidates, they may not be completely honest about their skills or interests—because they want to be hired—and employers' ability to find out the truth is limited. More than a generation ago the psychologist John Wanous proposed giving applicants a realistic preview of what the job is like. That still makes sense as a way to head off those who would end up being unhappy in the job. It's not surprising that Google has found a way to do this with gamification: Job seekers see what the work would be like by playing a game version of it. Marriott has done the same, even for low-level employees. Its My Marriott Hotel game targets young people in developing countries who may have had little experience in hotels to show them what it's like and to steer them to the recruiting site if they score well on the game. The key for any company, though, is that the preview should make clear what is difficult and challenging about the work as well as why it's fun so that candidates who don't fit won't apply.

It should be easy for candidates to learn about a company and a job, but making it really easy to apply, just to fill up that funnel, doesn't make much sense. During the dot-com boom Texas Instruments cleverly introduced a preemployment test that allowed applicants to see their scores before they applied. If their scores weren't high enough for the company to take their applications seriously, they tended not to proceed, and the company saved the cost of having to process their applications.

If the goal is to get better hires in a cost-effective manner, it's more important to scare away candidates who don't fit than to jam more candidates into the recruiting funnel.

Test candidates' standard skills

How to determine which candidates to hire—what predicts who will be a good employee—has been rigorously studied at least since World War I. The personnel psychologists who investigated this have learned much about predicting good hires that contemporary organizations have since forgotten, such as that neither college grades nor unstructured sequential interviews (hopping from office to office) are a good predictor, whereas past performance is.

Since it can be difficult (if not impossible) to glean sufficient information about an outside applicant's past performance, what other predictors are good? There is remarkably little consensus even among experts. That's mainly because a typical job can have so many tasks and aspects, and different factors predict success at different tasks.

There is general agreement, however, that testing to see whether individuals have standard skills is about the best we can do. Can the candidate speak French? Can she do simple programming tasks? And so forth. But just doing the tests is not enough. The economists Mitchell Hoffman, Lisa B. Kahn, and Danielle Li found that even when companies conduct such tests, hiring managers often ignore them—and when they do, they get worse hires. The psychologist Nathan Kuncel and colleagues discovered that even when hiring managers use objective criteria and tests, applying their own weights and judgment to those criteria leads them to pick worse candidates than if they had used a standard formula. Only 40% of employers, however, do any tests of skills or general abilities, including IQ. What are they doing instead? Seventy-four percent do drug tests, including for marijuana use; even employers in states where recreational use is now legal still seem to do so.

Be wary of vendors bearing high-tech gifts

Into the testing void has come a new group of entrepreneurs who either are data scientists or have them in tow. They bring a fresh approach to the hiring process—but often with little understanding of how hiring actually works. John Sumser, of HRExaminer, an online newsletter that focuses on HR technology, estimates that on average, companies get five to seven pitches *every day*—almost all of them about hiring—from vendors using data science to address HR issues. These vendors have all sorts of cool-sounding assessments, such as computer games that can be scored to predict who will be a good hire. We don't know whether any of these actually lead to better hires, because few of them are validated against actual job performance. That aside, these assessments have spawned a counterwave of vendors who help candidates learn how to score well on them. Lloyds Bank, for example, developed a virtual-reality-based assessment of candidate potential, and JobTestPrep offers to teach potential candidates how to do well on it. Especially for IT and technical jobs, cheating on skills tests and even video interviews (where colleagues off camera give help) is such a concern that eTeki and other specialized vendors help employers figure out who is cheating in real time.

Revamp your interviewing process

The amount of time employers spend on interviews has almost doubled since 2009, according to research from Glassdoor. How much of that increase represents delays in setting up those interviews is impossible to tell, but it provides at least a partial explanation for why it takes longer to fill jobs now. Interviews are arguably the most difficult technique to get right, because interviewers should stick to questions that predict good hires—mainly about past behavior or performance that's relevant to the tasks of the job—and ask them consistently across candidates. Just winging it and asking whatever comes to mind is next to useless.

More important, interviews are where biases most easily show up, because interviewers do usually decide on the fly what to ask of whom and how to interpret the answer. Everyone knows some executive who is absolutely certain he knows the one question that will really predict good candidates ("If you were stranded on a desert island. . ."). The sociologist Lauren Rivera's examination of interviews for elite positions, such as those in professional services firms, indicates that hobbies, particularly those associated with the rich, feature prominently as a selection criterion.

Interviews are most important for assessing "fit with our culture," which is the number one hiring criterion employers report using, according to research from the Rockefeller Foundation. It's also one of the squishiest attributes to measure, because few organizations have an accurate and consistent view of their own culture—and even if they do, understanding what attributes represent a good fit is not straightforward. For example, does the fact that an applicant belonged to a fraternity reflect experience working with others or elitism or bad attitudes toward women? Should it be completely irrelevant? Letting someone with no experience or training make such calls is a recipe for bad hires and, of course, discriminatory behavior. Think hard about whether your interviewing protocols make any sense and resist the urge to bring even more managers into the interview process.

Recognize the strengths and weaknesses of machine learning models

Culture fit is another area into which new vendors are swarming. Typically they collect data from current employees, create a machine learning model to predict the attributes of the best ones, and then use that model to hire candidates with the same attributes.

As with many other things in this new industry, that sounds good until you think about it; then it becomes replete with problems. Given the best performers of the past, the algorithm will almost certainly include *white* and *male* as key variables. If it's restricted from using that category, it will come up with attributes associated with being a white male, such as playing rugby.

Machine learning models do have the potential to find important but previously unconsidered relationships. Psychologists, who have dominated research on hiring, have been keen to study attributes relevant to their interests, such as personality, rather than asking the broader question "What identifies a potential good hire?" Their results gloss over the fact that they often have only a trivial ability to predict who will be a good performer, particularly when many factors are involved. Machine learning, in contrast, can come up with highly predictive factors. Research by Evolv, a workforce analytics pioneer (now part of Cornerstone OnDemand), found that expected commuting distance for the candidate predicted turnover very well. But that's not a question the psychological models thought to ask. (And even that question has problems.)

The advice on selection is straightforward: Test for skills. Ask assessments vendors to show evidence that they can actually predict who the good employees will be. Do fewer, more-consistent interviews.

Expanding the Pool: How Goldman Sachs Changed the Way It Recruits

by Dane E. Holmes

Goldman Sachs is a people-centric business—every day our employees engage with our clients to find solutions to their challenges. As a consequence, hiring extraordinary talent is vital to our success and can never be taken for granted. In the wake of the 2008 financial crisis we faced a challenge that was, frankly, relatively new to our now 150-

year-old firm. For decades investment banking had been one of the most sought-after, exciting, and fast-growing industries in the world. That made sense—we were growing by double digits and had high returns, which meant that opportunity and reward were in great supply. However, the crash took some of the sheen off our industry; both growth and returns moderated. And simultaneously, the battle for talent intensified—within and outside our industry. Many of the candidates we were pursuing were heading off to Silicon Valley, private equity, or start-ups. Furthermore, we were no longer principally looking for a specialized cadre of accounting, finance, and economics majors: New skills, especially coding, were in huge demand at Goldman Sachs—and pretty much everywhere else. The wind had shifted from our backs to our faces, and we needed to respond.

Not long ago the firm relied on a narrower set of factors for identifying the "best" students, such as school, GPA, major, leadership roles, and relevant experience—the classic résumé topics. No longer. We decided to replace our hiring playbook with emerging best practices for assessment and recruitment, so we put together a task force of senior business leaders, PhDs in industrial and organizational psychology, data scientists, and experts in recruiting. Some people asked, "Why overhaul a recruiting process that has proved so successful?" and "Don't you already have many more qualified applicants than available jobs?" These were reasonable questions. But often staying successful is about learning and changing rather than sticking to the tried-and-true.

Each year we hire up to 3,000 summer interns and nearly as many new analysts directly from campuses. In our eyes, these are the firm's future leaders, so it made sense to focus our initial reforms there. They involved two major additions to our campus recruiting strategy—video interviews and structured interviewing.

Asynchronous Video Interviews

Traditionally we had flown recruiters and business professionals to universities for first-round interviews. The schools would give us a set date and number of time slots to meet with students.

That is most definitely not a scalable model. It restricted us to a smaller number of campuses and only as many students as we could squeeze into a limited schedule. It also meant that we tended to focus on top-ranked schools. How many qualified candidates were at a school became more important than who were the most talented students regardless of their school. However, we knew that candidates didn't have to attend Harvard, Princeton, or Oxford to excel at Goldman Sachs—our leadership ranks were already rich with people from other schools. What's more, as we've built offices in new cities and geographic locations, we've needed to recruit at more schools located in those areas. Video interviews allow us to do that.

At a time when companies were just beginning to experiment with digital interviewing, we decided to use "asynchronous" video interviews—in which candidates record their answers to interview questions—for all first-round interactions with candidates. Our recruiters record standardized questions and send them to students, who have three days to return videos of their answers. This can be done on a computer or a mobile device. Our recruiters and business professionals review the videos to narrow the pool and then invite the selected applicants to a Goldman Sachs office for final-round, in-person interviews. (To create the video platform, we partnered with a company and built our own digital solution around its product.)

This approach has had a meaningful impact in two ways. First, with limited effort, we can now spend more time getting to know the people who apply for jobs at Goldman Sachs. In 2015, the year before we rolled out this platform, we interviewed fewer than 20% of all our campus applicants; in 2018 almost 40% of the students who applied to the firm participated in a first-round interview. Second, we now encounter talent from places we previously didn't get to. In 2015 we interviewed students from 798 schools around the world, compared with 1,268 for our most recent incoming class. In the United States, where the majority of our student hires historically came from "target schools," the opposite is now true. The top of our recruiting funnel is wider, and the output is more diverse.

Being a people-driven business, we have worked hard to ensure that the video interviews don't feel cold and impersonal. They are only one component of a broader process that makes up the Goldman Sachs recruitment experience. We still regularly send Goldman professionals to campuses to engage directly with students at informational sessions, "coffee chats," and other recruiting events. But now our goal is much more to share information than to assess candidates, because we want people to understand the firm and what it offers before they tell us why they want an internship or a job.

We also want them to be as well prepared as possible for our interview process. Our goal is a level playing field. To help achieve it, we've created tip sheets and instructions on preparing for a video interview. Because the platform doesn't allow videos to be edited once they've been recorded, we offer a practice question before the interview begins and a countdown before the questions are asked. We also give students a formal channel for escalating issues should technical problems arise, though that rarely occurs.

We're confident that this approach has created a better experience for recruits. It uses a medium they've grown up with (video), and most important, they can do their interviews when they feel fresh and at a time that works with their schedule. (Our data shows that they prefer Thursday or Sunday night—whereas our previous practice was to interview during working hours.) We suspected that if the process was a turnoff for applicants, we would see a dip in the percentage who accepted our interviews and our offers. That hasn't happened.

Structured Questioning and Assessments

How can you create an assessment process that not only helps select top talent but focuses on specific characteristics associated with success? Define it, structure it, and don't deviate from it. Research shows that structured interviews are effective at assessing candidates and helping predict job performance. So we ask candidates about specific experiences they've had that are similar to situations they may face at Goldman Sachs ("Tell me about a time when you were working on a project with someone who was not completing his or her tasks") and pose hypothetical scenarios they might encounter in the future ("In an elevator, you overhear confidential information about a coworker who is also a friend. The friend approaches you and asks if you've heard anything negative about him recently. What do you do?").

Essentially, we are focused less on past achievements and more on understanding whether a candidate has qualities that will positively affect our firm and our culture. Our structured interview questions are designed to assess candidates on 10 core competencies, including analytical thinking and integrity, which we know correlate with long-term success at the firm. They are evaluated on six competencies in the first round; if they progress, they're assessed on the remaining four during in-person interviews.

We have a rotating library of questions for each competency, along with a rubric for interviewers that explains how to rate responses on a five-point scale from "outstanding" to "poor." We also train our interviewers to conduct structured interviews, provide them with prep materials immediately before they interview a candidate, and run detailed calibration meetings using all the candidate data we've gathered throughout the recruiting process to ensure that certain interviewers aren't introducing grade inflation (or deflation). We're experimenting with prehire assessment tests to be paired with these interviews; we already offer a technical coding and math exam for applicants to our engineering organization.

We decided not to pilot these changes and instead rolled them out en masse, because we realized that buy-in would come from being able to show results quickly—and because we know that no process is perfect. Indeed, what I love most about our new approach is that we've turned our recruiting department into a laboratory for continuous learning and refinement. With more than 50,000 candidate video recordings, we're now sitting on a treasure trove of data that will help us conduct insightful analyses and answer questions necessary to run our business: Are we measuring the right competencies? Should some be weighted more heavily than others? What about the candidates' backgrounds? Which interviewers are most effective? Does a top-ranked student at a state school create more value for us than an average student from the Ivy League? We already have indications that students recruited from the new schools in our pool perform just as well as students from our traditional ones—and in some cases are more likely to stay longer at the firm.

What's next for our recruiting efforts? We receive almost 500,000 applications each year. From this pool we hire approximately 3%. We believe that many of the other 97% could be very successful at Goldman Sachs. As a result, picking the right 3% is less about just the individual and increasingly about matching the right person to the right role. That match may be made straight out of college or years later. We're experimenting with résumé-reading algorithms that will help candidates identify the business departments best suited to their skills and interests. We're looking at how virtual reality might help us better educate students about working in our offices and in our industry. And we're evaluating various tools and tests to bring even more data into the hiring decision process. Can I imagine a future in which companies rely exclusively on machines and algorithms to rate résumés and interviews? Maybe, for some. But I don't see us ever eliminating the human element at Goldman Sachs; it's too deeply embedded in our culture, in the work we do, and in what we believe drives success.

I'm excited to see where this journey takes us. Our 2019 campus class is shaping up to be the most diverse ever—and it's composed entirely of people who were selected through rigorous, objective assessments. There's no way we aren't better off as a result.

Data Science Can't Fix Hiring (Yet)

by Peter Cappelli

Recruiting managers desperately need new tools, because the existing ones—unstructured interviews, personality tests, personal referrals—aren't very effective. The newest development in hiring, which is both promising and worrying, is the rise of data science–driven algorithms to find and assess job candidates. By my count, more than 100 vendors are creating and selling these tools to companies. Unfortunately, data science—which is still in its infancy when it comes to recruiting and hiring—is not yet the panacea employers hope for.

Vendors of these new tools promise they will help reduce the role that social bias plays in hiring. And the algorithms can indeed help identify good job candidates who would previously have been screened out for lack of a certain education or social pedigree. But these tools may also identify and promote the use of predictive variables that are (or should be) troubling.

Because most data scientists seem to know so little about the context of employment, their tools are often worse than nothing. For instance, an astonishing percentage build their models by simply looking at attributes of the "best performers" in workplaces and then identifying which job candidates have the same attributes. They use anything that's easy to measure: facial expressions, word choice, comments on social media, and so forth. But a failure to check for any real difference between high-performing and low-performing employees on these attributes limits their usefulness. Furthermore, scooping up data from social media or the websites people have visited also raises important questions about privacy. True, the information can be accessed legally; but the individuals who created the postings didn't intend or authorize them to be used for such purposes. Furthermore, is it fair that something you posted as an undergrad can end up driving your hiring algorithm a generation later?

Another problem with machine learning approaches is that few employers collect the large volumes of data—number of hires, performance appraisals, and so on—that the algorithms require to make accurate predictions. Although vendors can theoretically overcome that hurdle by aggregating data from many employers, they don't really know whether individual company contexts are so distinct that predictions based on data from the many are inaccurate for the one.

Yet another issue is that all analytic approaches to picking candidates are backward looking, in the sense that they are based on outcomes that have already happened. (Algorithms are especially reliant on past experiences in part because building them requires lots and lots of observations—many years' worth of job performance data even for a large employer.) As Amazon learned, the past may be very different from the future you seek. It discovered that the hiring algorithm it had been working on since 2014 gave lower scores to women—even to attributes associated with women, such as participating in women's studies programs—because historically the best performers in the company had disproportionately been men. So the algorithm looked for people just like them. Unable to fix that problem, the company stopped using the algorithm in 2017. Nonetheless, many other companies are pressing ahead.

The underlying challenge for data scientists is that hiring is simply not like trying to predict, say, when a ball bearing will fail—a question for which any predictive measure might do. Hiring is so consequential that it is governed not just by legal frameworks but by fundamental notions of fairness. The fact that some criterion is associated with good job performance is necessary but not sufficient for using it in hiring.

Take a variable that data scientists have found to have predictive value: commuting distance to the job. According to the data, people with longer commutes suffer higher rates of attrition. However, commuting distance is governed by where you live—which is governed by housing prices, relates to income, and also relates to race. Picking whom to hire on the basis of where they live most likely has an adverse impact on protected groups such as racial minorities.

Unless no other criterion predicts at least as well as the one being used—and that is extremely difficult to determine in machine learning algorithms—companies violate the law if they use hiring criteria that have adverse impacts. Even then, to stay on the right side of the law, they must show why the criterion creates good performance. That might be possible in the case of commuting time, but—at least for the moment—it is not for facial expressions, social media postings, or other measures whose significance companies cannot demonstrate.

In the end, the drawback to using algorithms is that we're trying to use them on the cheap: building them by looking only at best performers rather than all performers, using only measures that are easy to gather, and relying on vendors' claims that the algorithms work elsewhere rather than observing the results with our own employees. Not only is there no free lunch here, but you might be better off skipping the cheap meal altogether.

The Way Forward

It's impossible to get better at hiring if you can't tell whether the candidates you select become good employees. If you don't know where you're going, any road will take you there. You must have a way to measure which employees are the best ones.

Why is that not getting through to companies? Surveyed employers say the main reason they don't examine whether their practices lead to better hires is that measuring employee performance is difficult. Surely this is a prime example of making the perfect the enemy of the good. Some aspects of performance are not difficult to measure: Do employees quit? Are they absent? Virtually all employers conduct performance appraisals. If you don't trust them, try something simpler. Ask supervisors, "Do you regret hiring this individual? Would you hire him again?"

Organizations that don't check to see how well their practices predict the quality of their hires are lacking in one of the most consequential aspects of modern business.

Originally published in May–June 2019. Reprint R1903B

How Dual-Career Couples Make It Work

by Jennifer Petriglieri

CAMILLE AND PIERRE MET in their early forties after each one's marriage had ended. Both were deeply committed to their careers and to their new relationship. Camille, an accountant, had felt pressured by her ex-husband to slow her progress toward partnership at her firm. Pierre, a production manager at an automotive company, was embroiled in a bitter divorce from his wife, who had given up her career to accommodate the geographic moves that his required. (As with the other couples I've profiled in this article, these aren't their real names.) Bruised by their past experiences, they agreed to place their careers on an equal footing. Initially things went smoothly, but two years in, Camille began to feel trapped on a professional path that she realized she had chosen because "that was what the smart kids did."

Mindful of their pact, Pierre calmly listened to her doubts and encouraged her to explore alternatives. But as the months wore on, he began to feel weighed down as he juggled providing emotional support to Camille, navigating their complex family logistics (both had children from their former marriages), and succeeding in his demanding job. When he began to question his own career direction, he wondered how the two of them could manage to change course. They couldn't afford to take time out from work, nor could they take much time to reflect and keep their family and relationship afloat.

Frustrated and exhausted, both wondered how they could continue to find meaning and fulfillment in their lives.

Dual-earner couples are on the rise. According to Pew Research, in 63% of couples with children in the United States, for example, both partners work (this figure is slightly higher in the EU). Many of these are *dual-career couples:* Both partners are highly educated, work full-time in demanding professional or managerial jobs, and see themselves on an upward path in their roles. For these couples, as for Pierre and Camille, work is a primary source of identity and a primary channel for ambition. Evidence is mounting from sociological research that when both partners dedicate themselves to work and to home life, they reap benefits such as increased economic freedom, a more satisfying relationship, and a lower-than-average chance of divorce.

Because their working lives and personal lives are deeply intertwined, however, dual-career couples face unique challenges. How do they decide whose job to relocate for, when it's OK for one partner to make a risky career change, or who will leave work early to pick up a sick child from school? How can they give family commitments—and each other—their full attention while both of them are working in demanding roles? And when one of them wants to undertake a professional reinvention, what does that mean for the other? They must work out these questions together, in a way that lets both thrive in love and work. If they don't, regrets and imbalances quickly build up, threatening to hinder their careers, dissolve their relationship, or both.

Many of these challenges are well recognized, and I've previously written in HBR about how companies can adapt their talent strategies to account for some of them ("Talent Management and the Dual-Career Couple," May–June 2018). But for the couples themselves, little guidance is available. Most advice treats major career decisions as if one is flying solo, without a partner, children, or aging parents to consider. When it's for couples, it focuses on their relationship, not how that intersects with their professional dreams, or it addresses how to balance particular trade-offs, such as careers versus family, or how to prioritize partners' work travel. What couples

Idea in Brief

The Problem

When both members of a couple have demanding careers, their work and personal lives are deeply intertwined—and often at odds.

The Transitions

Dual-career couples tend to go through three phases of being particularly vulnerable: when they first learn to work together as a couple; when they experience a midlife reinvention; and in the final stages of their working lives.

The Solution

Couples who communicate at each transition about values, boundaries, and fears have a good chance of being fulfilled both in their relationships and in their careers.

need is a more comprehensive approach for managing the moments when commitments and aspirations clash.

My personal experience in a dual-career couple, and my realization that little systematic academic research had been done in this area, prompted a six-year investigation into the lives of more than 100 dual-career couples, resulting in my book, *Couples That Work*. The people I studied come from around the world, range in age from mid-twenties to mid-sixties, and represent a range of professions, from corporate executive to entrepreneur to worker in the nonprofit sector. (See the sidebar "About the Research.") My research revealed that dual-career couples overcome their challenges by directly addressing deeper psychological and social forces—such as struggles for power and control; personal hopes, fears, and losses; and assumptions and cultural expectations about the roles partners should play in each other's lives and what it means to have a good relationship or career.

I also discovered that three transition points typically occur during dual-career couples' working and love lives, when those forces are particularly strong. It is during these transitions, I found, that some couples craft a way to thrive in love and work, while others are plagued by conflict and regret. By understanding each transition and knowing what questions to ask each other and what traps to avoid, dual-career couples can emerge stronger, fulfilled in their relationships and in their careers.

About the Research

I STUDIED 113 DUAL-CAREER COUPLES. They ranged in age from 26 to 63, with an even distribution among age groups. The majority of couples—76—were in their first significant partnership. Participants in the study came from 32 countries on four continents, and their ethnic and religious backgrounds reflected this diversity. At the time of the study, roughly 35% resided in North America, 40% in Europe, and 25% in the rest of the world. In 68 of the couples at least one partner had children. Eleven of the couples identified as gay, and the rest as straight. Just under 60% of the participants were pursuing careers in the corporate world. The others were spread roughly equally among the professions (such as medicine, law, and academia), entrepreneurship, government, and the nonprofit sector.

I interviewed the members of each couple separately, asking them about the development of their relationships, their career paths, their interactions as a couple, and their family and friend networks.

Transition 1: Working as a Couple

When Jamal and Emily met, in their late twenties, trade-offs were the last thing on their minds. They were full of energy, optimistic, and determined to live life to the fullest. Jamal, a project manager in a civil engineering firm, traveled extensively for work and was given increasingly complex projects to lead, while Emily, who worked at a clothing company, had just been promoted to her first management role. They saw each other mostly on weekends, which they often spent on wilderness hiking adventures. They married 18 months after their first date.

Then, in the space of three months, their world changed dramatically. While Emily was pregnant with their first child, Jamal's boss asked him to run a critical infrastructure project in Mexico. Jamal agreed to spend three weeks out of every month in Mexico City; designating some of his pay raise to extra child care would allow Emily to keep working in Houston, where they lived. But when their daughter, Aisha, was born two weeks early, Jamal was stuck in the Mexico City airport waiting for a flight home. Soon Emily, who was single-handedly managing Aisha, her job, and their home, discovered that the additional child care wasn't enough; she felt overburdened and unappreciated. Jamal was exhausted by the relentless travel and the stress of the giant new project; he felt isolated, incompetent, and guilty.

After many arguments, they settled on what they hoped was a practical solution: Because Jamal earned more, Emily took a smaller project role that she could manage remotely, and she and Aisha joined him in Mexico. But Emily felt disconnected from her company's head office and was passed over for a promotion, and eventually she grew resentful of the arrangement. By the time Jamal's boss began talking about his next assignment, their fighting had become intense.

The first transition that dual-career couples must navigate often comes as a response to the first major life event they face together—typically a big career opportunity, the arrival of a child, or the merger of families from previous relationships. To adapt, the partners must negotiate how to prioritize their careers and divide family commitments. Doing so in a way that lets them both thrive requires an underlying shift: They must move from having parallel, independent careers and lives to having interdependent ones.

My research shows two common traps for couples negotiating their way through their first transition:

Concentrating exclusively on the practical

In the first transition in particular, couples often look for logistical solutions to their challenges, as Jamal and Emily did when they arranged for extra child care and negotiated how many weekends Jamal would be home. This focus is understandable—such problems are tangible, and the underlying psychological and social tensions are murky and anxiety provoking—but it prolongs the struggle, because those tensions remain unresolved.

Instead of simply negotiating over calendars and to-do lists, couples must understand, share, and discuss the emotions, values, and fears underlying their decisions. Talking about feelings as well as practicalities can help them mitigate and manage them.

Basing decisions primarily on money

Many couples focus on economic gain as they decide where to live, whose career to prioritize, and who will do the majority of the child care. But as sensible (and sometimes unavoidable) as this is, it often

A Guide to Couple Contracting

DRAWING ON MY RESEARCH, I've developed a systematic tool to help dual-career couples who are facing any of the three transitions described in this article. I call it couple contracting, because to shape their joint path, partners must address three areas—values, boundaries, and fears—and find common ground in each. Values define the direction of your path, boundaries set its borders, and fears reveal the potential cliffs to avoid on either side. Sharing a clear view in these three domains will make it easier to negotiate and overcome the challenges you encounter together.

First, take some time on your own to write down your thoughts about each of the three areas. Then share your reflections with each other. Listen to and acknowledge each other's responses, resisting any temptation to diminish or discount your partner's fears. Next, note where you have common ground and where your values and boundaries diverge. No couple has perfect overlap in those two areas, but if they are too divergent, negotiate a middle ground. If, for example, one of you could tolerate living apart for a period but the other could not, you'll need to shape a boundary that works for both of you.

Values

When our choices and actions align with our values, we feel content; when they don't, we feel stressed and unhappy. Openly discussing your values will make it easier to make choices that align with them. For example, if you and your partner know you both greatly value family time, you'll be clear that neither of you should take a job requiring 70-hour workweeks.

Questions to ask each other

What makes you happy and proud? What gives you satisfaction? What makes for a good life?

---

means that their decisions end up at odds with their other values and desires.

Few people live for financial gain alone. In their careers they are also motivated by continual learning and being given greater responsibilities. Outside work, they want to spend time with their children and pursue personal interests. Couples may be attracted to a location because of proximity to extended family, the quality

Boundaries

Setting clear boundaries together allows you to make big decisions more easily. Consider three types of boundaries: place, time, and presence.

Questions to ask each other

Are there places where you'd love to work and live at some point in your life? Are there places you'd prefer to avoid? Understanding that we may sometimes have to put in more hours than we'd like, how much work is too much? How would you feel about our taking jobs in different cities and living apart for a period? For how long? How much work travel is too much, and how will we juggle travel between us?

Fears

Monitoring each other's fears can help you spot trouble and take preventive action before your relationship enters dangerous territory. Many fears are endemic to relationships and careers: You may worry that your partner's family will encroach on your relationship, that over time the two of you will grow apart, that your partner will have an affair, that you will have to sacrifice your career for your partner's, or that you may not be able to have children. But sharing these fears allows you to build greater empathy and support. If you know that your partner is worried about the role of your parents in your lives, for example, you are more likely to manage the boundary between them and your partnership sensitively. Likewise, if you are interested in a risky career transition but worried that financial commitments would prevent it, you might agree to cut back on family spending in order to build a buffer.

Questions to ask each other

What are your concerns for the future? What's your biggest fear about how our relationship and careers interact? What do you dread might happen in our lives?

---

of life it affords, or their ability to build a strong community. Basing the decision to move to Mexico on Jamal's higher salary meant that he and Emily ignored their other interests, feeding their discontent.

Couples who are successful discuss the foundations and the structure of their joint path forward. First, they must come to some agreement on core aspects of their relationship: their values, boundaries, and fears. (See the sidebar "A Guide to Couple Contracting.") Negotiating and finding common ground in these areas helps them navigate difficult decisions because they can agree on criteria in advance. Doing this together is important; couples that make this arrangement work, I found, make choices openly and jointly, rather than implicitly and for each other. The ones I studied who had never addressed their core criteria struggled in later transitions, because those criteria never go away.

Next, couples must discuss how to prioritize their careers and divide family commitments. Striving for 50/50 is not always the best option; neither must one decide to always give the other's career priority.

There are three basic models to consider: (1) In *primary-secondary,* one partner's career takes priority over the other's for the duration of their working lives. The primary person dedicates more time to work and less to the family, and his or her professional commitments (and geographic requirements) usually come before the secondary person's. (2) In *turn taking,* the partners agree to periodically swap the primary and secondary positions. (3) In *double-primary,* they continually juggle two primary careers.

My research shows that couples can feel fulfilled in their careers and relationships whichever model they pursue, as long as it aligns with their values and they openly discuss and explicitly agree on their options. Couples who pursue the third option are often the most successful, although it's arguably the most difficult, precisely because they are forced to address conflicts most frequently.

To work past their deadlock, Emily and Jamal finally discussed what really mattered to them beyond financial success. They identified pursuit of their chosen careers, proximity to nature, and a stable home for Aisha where they could both actively parent her. They admitted their fears of growing apart, and in response agreed to an important restriction: They would live in the same city and would limit work travel to 25% of their time. They agreed to place their geographic boundaries around North America, and Jamal suggested that they both draw circles on a map around the cities where they felt they could make a home and have two careers. Their conversations and mapping exercise eventually brought them to a resolution—and a new start in Atlanta, where they would pursue a double-primary model. Three years later they are progressing in their careers, happy in their family life, and expecting a second child.

Transition 2: Reinventing Themselves

Psychological theory holds that early in life many people follow career and personal paths that conform to the expectations of their parents, friends, peers, and society, whereas in their middle years many feel a pressing need for *individuation*, or breaking free of those expectations to become authors of their own lives. This tends to happen in people's forties, regardless of their relationship status, and is part of a process colloquially known as the midlife crisis.

We tend to think of a midlife crisis mostly in personal terms (a husband leaves his wife, for example, and buys a sports car), but in dual-career couples, the intense focus on professional success means that the partners' job tracks come under scrutiny as well. This combined personal and professional crisis forms the basis of the second transition. Camille and Pierre, whose story began this article, were in the midst of it.

As each partner wrestles with self-redefinition, the two often bump up against long-settled arrangements they have made and the identities, relationship, and careers they have crafted together. Some of those arrangements—whose career takes precedence, for example—may need to be reconsidered to allow one partner to quit a job and explore alternatives. It may be painful to question the choices they made together during the previous transition and have since built their lives around. This can be threatening to a relationship; it's not uncommon for one partner to interpret the other's desire to rethink past career choices as an inclination to rethink the relationship as well, or even to potentially end it. Couples who handle this transition well find ways to connect with and support each other through what can feel like a very solitary process.

The second transition often begins—as it did for Camille and Pierre—when one partner reexamines a career or life path. That person must reflect on questions such as: What led me to this impasse? Why did I make the choices I made? Who am I? What do I desire from life? Whom do I want to become? He or she should also take time to explore alternative paths, through networking events, job shadowing, secondments, volunteer work, and so forth. Such individual reflection and exploration can lead couples to the first trap of the second transition:

Mistrust and defensiveness

Living with a partner who is absorbed in exploring new paths can feel threatening. Painful questions surface: Why is my partner not satisfied? Is this a career problem or a relationship problem? Am I to blame? Why does he or she need new people? Am I no longer enough? These doubts can lead to mistrust and defensiveness, which may push the exploring partner to withdraw further from the relationship, making the other even more mistrustful and defensive, until eventually the relationship itself becomes an obstacle to individuation, rather than a space for it.

In such a situation, people should first be open about their concerns and let their partners reassure them that the angst is not about them or the relationship. Next, they should adopt what literary critics call *suspension of disbelief*—that is, faith that the things they have doubts about will unfold in interesting ways and are worth paying attention to. This attitude will both enrich their own lives and make their partners' exploration easier.

Finally, they should understand their role as supporters. Psychologists call this role in a relationship the *secure base* and see it as vital to the other partner's growth. Originally identified and described by the psychologist John Bowlby, the secure base allows us to stretch ourselves by stepping outside our comfort zone while someone by our side soothes our anxieties about doing so. Without overly interfering, supporters should encourage their partners' exploration and reflection, even if it means moving away from the comfortable relationship they've already established.

Being a secure base for a partner presents its own trap, however:

Asymmetric support

In some couples one partner consistently supports the other without receiving support in return. That's what happened to Camille and Pierre. Pierre's experience in his former marriage, in which his wife gave up her career for his, made him determined to support Camille, and he initially stepped up to be a secure base for her. Their lives were so packed, however, that Camille had trouble finding the energy to return the favor. The result was that her exploration and reflection became an impediment to Pierre's, creating a developmental and relationship deadlock. It is important to remember that acting as a secure base does not mean annihilating your own wishes, atoning for past selfishness, or being perfect. You can be a wonderful supporter for your partner while requesting support in return and taking time for yourself. In fact, that will most likely make you a far better (and less resentful) supporter.

In my research I found that couples who make it through their second transition are those in which the partners encourage each other to do this work—even if it means that one of them is exploring and providing support at the same time.

Once the exploring partner has had a chance to determine what he or she wants in a career, a life, or a relationship, the next step is to make it happen—as a couple. Couples need to renegotiate the roles they play in each other's lives. Take Matthew and James, another pair I spoke with, who had risen through the professional ranks in their 18 years together. When Matthew realized that he wanted to get off what he called the success train—on which he felt like a mere passenger—both he and James had to let go of their identity as a power couple and revisit the career-prioritization agreement they had forged during their first transition. Initially Matthew was reluctant to talk to James about his doubts, because he questioned whether James would still love him if he changed direction. When they started discussing this, however, they realized that their identity as a power couple had trapped them in a dynamic in which both needed to succeed but neither could outshine the other.

Acknowledging and renegotiating this unspoken arrangement allowed James to shoot for his first senior executive position and Matthew to transition into the nonprofit sector. The time and care they took to answer their existential questions and renegotiate the roles they played in each other's lives set them up for a renewed period of growth in their careers and in their relationship.

Transition 3: Loss and Opportunity

Attending her mother's funeral was one of the most difficult experiences of Norah's life. It was the culmination of two years of immense change for her and her husband, Jeremy, who were in their late fifties. The change began when their fathers unexpectedly passed away within five weeks of each other, and they became caregivers for Norah's ailing mother just as their children were leaving the nest and their own careers were in flux.

Jeremy is a digital visual artist. His studio's main projects were ending because a big client was moving on. Though he was sad, he had become confident enough to feel excited about whatever might come next. Norah had been working for the same small agricultural machinery business for 26 years; she had once wanted to change careers but felt that she couldn't do so while Jeremy was relying on her for emotional and logistical support. Now she was being asked to take an early retirement deal. She felt thrown on the scrap heap despite her long commitment to the company. No career, no parents, no children to care for—who was she now? She felt disoriented and adrift.

The third transition is typically triggered by shifting roles later in life, which often create a profound sense of loss. Careers plateau or decline; bodies are no longer what they once were; children, if there are any, leave home. Sometimes one partner's career is going strong while the other's begins to ebb. Having raced through decades of career growth and child-rearing, couples wake up with someone who may have changed since the time they fell in love. They may both feel that way. These changes again raise fundamental questions of identity: Who am I now? Who do I want to be for the rest of my life?

Although loss usually triggers it, the third transition heralds opportunity. Chances for late-in-life reinvention abound, especially in today's world. Life expectancy is rising across the globe, and older couples may have several decades of reasonably good health and freedom from intensive parenting responsibilities. As careers and work become more flexible, especially for those with experience, people can engage in multiple activities more easily than previous generations could—combining advisory or consulting work with board service, for example. Their activities often include giving back to the community, leaving some kind of legacy, mentoring younger generations, rediscovering passions of their youth, or dedicating themselves more to friendships.

Their task in the third transition is to again reinvent themselves—this time in a way that is both grounded in past accomplishments and optimistic about possibilities for the future. They must mourn the old, welcome the new, figure out how the two fit together, and adjust their life path to support who they want to become.

One thing that struck me when I spoke to couples in their third transition is that it's most powerful when partners reinvent themselves together—not just reflecting jointly, as in the other transitions, but actually taking on a new activity or project side by side. When one is curious about a partner's life and work as well as one's own, an immense capacity for mutual revitalization is unlocked. I met many couples who were charting new paths out of this transition that involved a merging of their work—launching a new business together, for example.

The third transition also has its traps:

Unfinished business

For better or for worse, earlier relational patterns, approaches, decisions, and assumptions will influence how a couple's third transition unfolds. I found that the most common challenge in managing this transition was overcoming regret about perceived failures in the way the partners had "worked" as a couple—how they had prioritized their careers, or how each partner had supported the other's development (or not).

To move through the third transition, couples must acknowledge how they got where they are and commit to playing new roles for each other in the future. For example, Norah and Jeremy had become stuck in a pattern in which Norah was Jeremy's supporter. By recognizing this—and both their roles in cementing it—they were able to become more mutually supportive.

Narrow horizons

By the time a couple reaches the third transition, they will probably have suffered their fair share of disappointments and setbacks. They may be tired from years of taking care of others, or just from staying on the treadmill. As their roles shift and doubts about their identities grow, reinvention may be beyond consideration. In addition, because previous generations retired earlier, didn't live as long, and didn't have access to the gig economy, many couples lack role models for what reinvention can look like at this stage of life. If they don't deliberately broaden their horizons, they miss opportunities to discover themselves anew.

So couples must explore again. Even more than in the second transition, they need to flirt with multiple possibilities. Like healthy children, who are curious about the world, themselves, and those around them, they can actively seek new experiences and experiment, avoid taking things for granted, and constantly ask "Why?" Most of us suppress our childhood curiosity as life progresses and responsibilities pile up. But it is vital to overcome the fear of leaving behind a cherished self and allow ambitions and priorities to diversify. Exploring at this stage is rejuvenating.

Shifts in people's roles and identities offer a perfect excuse to question their current work, life, and loves. Many people associate exploring with looking for new options, which is surely important. But it's also about questioning assumptions and approaches and asking, "Is this really how things need to be?"

Having rebalanced their support for each other, Norah and Jeremy could open up to new possibilities. Having earned financial security from their previous work, they sought reinvention not only in their careers but also in their wider roles in the world. Encouraging each other, they both transitioned to portfolio working lives. Jeremy became a freelance digital visual artist, took a part-time role teaching young art students at a local college, and dedicated more time to his passion of dinghy sailing. Norah retrained to be a counselor working with distressed families and began volunteering at a local agricultural museum. With these new opportunities and more time for each other and their friends, they felt newfound satisfaction with their work and with their relationship.

The challenges couples face at each transition are different but linked. In their first transition, the partners accommodate to a major life event by negotiating the roles they will play in each other's lives. Over time those roles become constraining and spark the restlessness and questioning that lead to the second transition. To successfully navigate the third transition, couples must address regrets and developmental asymmetries left over from their first two transitions.

No one right path or solution exists for meeting these challenges. Although the 50/50 marriage—in which housework and child care are divided equally between the partners, and their careers are perfectly synced—may seem like a noble ideal, my research suggests that instead of obsessively trying to maintain an even "score," dual-career couples are better off being relentlessly curious, communicative, and proactive in making choices about combining their lives.

The Spouse Factor

by Jane Stevenson

Performing well as a high-level recruiter requires understanding what makes your candidates tick—and not just at work. That's especially true if I'm asking them to consider a job that requires relocation. In many cases I already know something about a candidate's family life—including the spouse's or partner's professional status, the ages of their kids (if any), and whether they have elderly parents living nearby. In cases where I don't know, I find a way to ask, "Is there anything in your family situation we should be sensitive to?" If there is, it's important to know early on, especially if these issues could become "blockers."

In my 34 years of experience, the most difficult factor to overcome when recruiting a candidate who has to relocate for a new job has been children, especially those in high school or with special needs. (This is often true whether the candidate is married or divorced; moving can be especially hard for someone who shares custody with an ex.) Spouses are the second most frequent reason a candidate will be reluctant to relocate, especially if he or she is part of a couple in which both are pursuing ambitious professional paths.

When I'm trying to recruit one member of a dual-career couple, it's important to fully understand the other's career, and also the city to which I hope to relocate them. For so-called trailing spouses, the most challenging careers are physician or lawyer in private practice or owner of a business that isn't portable. People in these situations have often spent years building a client base and a local reputation, and it's difficult to reproduce those in a new region. The size of the destination city is also a factor. If the candidate's partner works in a traditional corporate function, he or she will have an easier time finding a similar (or better) position in a big market like Los Angeles or New York than in a smaller city. If the trailing spouse travels frequently for work, being near a major airport is also vital.

If the candidate's partner won't or can't move, I'll often ask whether the couple would consider a "commuter marriage." Companies today are increasingly willing to let high-performing leaders commute or work remotely. However, they are much more willing to allow an existing employee to do so, because they know the person's track record; the risk feels higher with a new employee.

Sometimes we have to think creatively. A few years ago a colleague and I were recruiting a female candidate who was based in Europe for a job in Asia. She had a long-term partner who had a great job and was unwilling to move to Asia. So we looked at the likely career path of the candidate (if she took the new role) and concluded that if she did a great job in Asia, she'd most likely be promoted to a position at headquarters in the United States, where her partner *was* willing to move. So the two commuted for a couple of years, and then the woman I'd recruited did get a top job at headquarters; her partner moved to the United States, bringing them back together.

My work gives me a unique window onto how couples manage these situations, but my views are also informed by a research project I led at Korn Ferry on the careers of female CEOs. We interviewed 57 current or former CEOs about their paths to the corner office, and the most striking takeaway was the importance of strong spousal support for women who aspire to top jobs. When discussing the factors that led to their success, most of the women spontaneously brought up their husbands' support. About half the CEOs had spouses with substantial careers; managing their dual careers involved complex calendar negotiations, turn taking, weighing of career decisions, a willingness to relocate, and significant help from housekeepers, nannies, and so forth. About a third had spouses or partners who, by the time the women became CEOs, were assuming primary responsibility for home and children; some were househusbands, and others were retired or worked part-time.

Each of us has only so much energy to utilize, and dealing with a partner who isn't truly rooting for you professionally saps that energy, limiting your potential. A few of the CEOs we interviewed said they had previously had unsupportive husbands or partners but ultimately went on to connect with more-supportive ones. They speculated that they wouldn't have attained the top job if they hadn't received the support they needed. (Most male CEOs I've worked with say the same thing.) My children are now 24 and 21, and I tell them very bluntly: Choosing a spouse may be one of the most important career decisions you'll ever make, because that person will be either a support or a hindrance to your professional ambitions. So choose wisely.

I empathize with couples who struggle with these issues, because I've faced them myself. My husband is a pathologist. We've been married 37 years. For roughly the first two decades, his career took priority. We moved several times to accommodate his medical school training, residency, fellowships, and stint with the U.S. Air Force. I believe a sturdy flower can bloom anywhere, so I tried to look at those moves as opportunities: When we moved from California to Philadelphia, my job search led me to executive recruiting. When we moved to Texas, where my then employer had no office, I opened a new one, which was great experience. As my career has evolved, we've made changes. My travel schedule is insane. In 2007, when our children were much younger, my husband left his hospital job and started consulting to have more flexibility and to be more available for the kids. Since then we've considered my career the priority.

Having experienced this push and pull, I recognize that it's typically a phone call from someone like me—followed by a great job offer—that causes a couple to rethink their coequal arrangement. Very often, the resulting conversation will focus on the upside opportunity. It's natural for partners to compare the potential of their careers and decide to prioritize the one with the higher ROI. In the past that was typically the man's, but today it's frequently the woman's.

At such moments, many dual-career couples will decide that one career has to take a backseat, or that the lesser-earning partner will make a leap of faith and hope that he or she can find (or create) a great job in a new city. When couples face this prospect, I remind them that choosing to prioritize one partner's career doesn't mean it will be that way forever. Careers are long. The partner who's stepping back right now may be able to step forward in the future. I like to think I have credibility when I make this argument, because I've experienced that shift myself.

Originally published in September–October 2019. Reprint R1905B

Building the AI-Powered Organization

by Tim Fountaine, Brian McCarthy, and Tamim Saleh

ARTIFICIAL INTELLIGENCE IS reshaping business—though not at the blistering pace many assume. True, AI is now guiding decisions on everything from crop harvests to bank loans, and once pie-in-the-sky prospects such as totally automated customer service are on the horizon. The technologies that enable AI, like development platforms and vast processing power and data storage, are advancing rapidly and becoming increasingly affordable. The time seems ripe for companies to capitalize on AI. Indeed, we estimate that AI will add $13 trillion to the global economy over the next decade.

Yet, despite the promise of AI, many organizations' efforts with it are falling short. We've surveyed thousands of executives about how their companies use and organize for AI and advanced analytics, and our data shows that only 8% of firms engage in core practices that support widespread adoption. Most firms have run only ad hoc pilots or are applying AI in just a single business process.

Why the slow progress? At the highest level, it's a reflection of a failure to rewire the organization. In our surveys and our work with hundreds of clients, we've seen that AI initiatives face formidable cultural and organizational barriers. But we've also seen that leaders who at the outset take steps to break down those barriers can effectively capture AI's opportunities.

Making the Shift

One of the biggest mistakes leaders make is to view AI as a plug-and-play technology with immediate returns. Deciding to get a few projects up and running, they begin investing millions in data infrastructure, AI software tools, data expertise, and model development. Some of the pilots manage to eke out small gains in pockets of organizations. But then months or years pass without bringing the big wins executives expected. Firms struggle to move from the pilots to companywide programs—and from a focus on discrete business problems, such as improved customer segmentation, to big business challenges, like optimizing the entire customer journey.

Leaders also often think too narrowly about AI requirements. While cutting-edge technology and talent are certainly needed, it's equally important to align a company's culture, structure, and ways of working to support broad AI adoption. But at most businesses that aren't born digital, traditional mindsets and ways of working run counter to those needed for AI.

To scale up AI, companies must make three shifts:

From siloed work to interdisciplinary collaboration

AI has the biggest impact when it's developed by cross-functional teams with a mix of skills and perspectives. Having business and operational people work side by side with analytics experts will ensure that initiatives address broad organizational priorities, not just isolated business issues. Diverse teams can also think through the operational changes new applications may require—they're likelier to recognize, say, that the introduction of an algorithm that predicts maintenance needs should be accompanied by an overhaul of maintenance workflows. And when development teams involve end users in the design of applications, the chances of adoption increase dramatically.

Idea in Brief

The Problem

Many companies' efforts to scale up artificial intelligence fall short. That's because only 8% of firms are engaging in core practices that support widespread adoption.

The Solution

Cutting-edge technology and talent are not enough. Companies must break down organizational and cultural barriers that stand in AI's way.

The Leadership Imperatives

Leaders must convey the urgency of AI initiatives and their benefits for all; spend at least as much on adoption as on technology; organize AI work on the basis of the company's AI maturity, business complexity, and innovation pace; and invest in AI education for everyone.

From experience-based, leader-driven decision making to data-driven decision making at the front line

When AI is adopted broadly, employees up and down the hierarchy will augment their own judgment and intuition with algorithms' recommendations to arrive at better answers than either humans or machines could reach on their own. But for this approach to work, people at all levels have to trust the algorithms' suggestions and feel empowered to make decisions—and that means abandoning the traditional top-down approach. If employees have to consult a higher-up before taking action, that will inhibit the use of AI.

Decision processes shifted dramatically at one organization when it replaced a complex manual method for scheduling events with a new AI system. Historically, the firm's event planners had used colored tags, pins, and stickers to track conflicts, participants' preferences, and other considerations. They'd often relied on gut instinct and on input from senior managers, who also were operating on their instincts, to make decisions. The new system rapidly analyzed the vast range of scheduling permutations, using first one algorithm to distill hundreds of millions of options into millions of scenarios, and then another algorithm to boil down those millions into just hundreds, ranking the optimal schedules for each participant. Experienced human planners then applied their expertise to make final decisions supported by the data, without the need to get input from their leaders. The planners adopted the tool readily, trusting its output because they'd helped set its parameters and constraints and knew that they themselves would make the final call.

From rigid and risk-averse to agile, experimental, and adaptable

Organizations must shed the mindset that an idea needs to be fully baked or a business tool must have every bell and whistle before it's deployed. On the first iteration, AI applications rarely have all their desired functionality. A test-and-learn mentality will reframe mistakes as a source of discoveries, reducing the fear of failure. Getting early user feedback and incorporating it into the next version will allow firms to correct minor issues before they become costly problems. Development will speed up, enabling small AI teams to create minimum viable products in a matter of weeks rather than months.

Such fundamental shifts don't come easily. They require leaders to prepare, motivate, and equip the workforce to make a change. But leaders must first be prepared themselves. We've seen failure after failure caused by the lack of a foundational understanding of AI among senior executives. (Further on, we'll discuss how analytics academies can help leaders acquire that understanding.)

Setting Up for Success

To get employees on board and smooth the way for successful AI launches, leaders should devote early attention to several tasks:

Explaining why

A compelling story helps organizations understand the urgency of change initiatives and how all will benefit from them. This is particularly critical with AI projects, because fear that AI will take away jobs increases employees' resistance to it.

Leaders have to provide a vision that rallies everyone around a common goal. Workers must understand why AI is important to the business and how they'll fit into a new, AI-oriented culture. In particular, they need reassurance that AI will enhance rather than diminish or even eliminate their roles. (Our research shows that the majority of workers will need to adapt to using AI rather than be replaced by AI.)

When a large retail conglomerate wanted to get its employees behind its AI strategy, management presented it as an existential imperative. Leaders described the threat that digital retailers posed and how AI could help fend it off by improving the firm's operational efficiency and responsiveness. By issuing a call to arms in a fight for survival, management underscored the critical role that employees had to play.

In sharing their vision, the company's leaders put a spotlight on workers who had piloted a new AI tool that helped them optimize stores' product assortments and increase revenue. That inspired other workers to imagine how AI could augment and elevate their performance.

Anticipating unique barriers to change

Some obstacles, such as workers' fear of becoming obsolete, are common across organizations. But a company's culture may also have distinctive characteristics that contribute to resistance. For example, if a company has relationship managers who pride themselves on being attuned to customer needs, they may reject the notion that a machine could have better ideas about what customers want and ignore an AI tool's tailored product recommendations. And managers in large organizations who believe their status is based on the number of people they oversee might object to the decentralized decision making or reduction in reports that AI could allow.

In other cases, siloed processes can inhibit the broad adoption of AI. Organizations that assign budgets by function or business unit may struggle to assemble interdisciplinary agile teams, for example.

Some solutions can be found by reviewing how past change initiatives overcame barriers. Others may involve aligning AI initiatives with the very cultural values that seem like obstacles. At one financial institution with a strong emphasis on relationship banking, for example, leaders highlighted AI's ability to enhance ties with customers. The bank created a booklet for relationship managers that showed how combining their expertise and skills with AI's tailored product recommendations could improve customers' experiences and increase revenue and profit. The AI adoption program also included a contest for sales conversions driven by using the new tool; the winners' achievements were showcased in the CEO's monthly newsletter to employees.

A relatively new class of expert, analytics translators, can play a role in identifying roadblocks. These people bridge the data engineers and scientists from the technical realm with the people from the business realm—marketing, supply chain, manufacturing, risk personnel, and so on. Translators help ensure that the AI applications developed address business needs and that adoption goes smoothly. Early in the implementation process, they may survey end users, observe their habits, and study workflows to diagnose and fix problems.

Understanding the barriers to change can not only inform leaders about how to communicate with the workforce but also help them determine where to invest, what AI initiatives are most feasible, what training should be offered, what incentives may be necessary, and more.

Budgeting as much for integration and adoption as for technology (if not more)

In one of our surveys nearly 90% of the companies that had engaged in successful scaling practices had spent more than half of their analytics budgets on activities that drove adoption, such as workflow redesign, communication, and training. Only 23% of the remaining companies had committed similar resources.

Consider one telecom provider that was launching a new AI-driven customer-retention program in its call center. The company invested simultaneously in AI model development and in helping the center's employees transition to the new approach. Instead of just reacting to calls canceling service, they would proactively reach out to customers at risk of defection, giving them AI-generated recommendations on new offers they'd be likely to accept. The employees got training and on-the-job coaching in the sales skills needed to close the business. Coaches and managers listened in on their calls, gave them individualized feedback, and continually updated the training materials and call scripts. Thanks to those coordinated efforts, the new program reduced customer attrition by 10%.

Balancing feasibility, time investment, and value

Pursuing initiatives that are unduly difficult to implement or require more than a year to launch can sabotage both current and future AI projects.

Organizations needn't focus solely on quick wins; they should develop a portfolio of initiatives with different time horizons. Automated processes that don't need human intervention, such as AI-assisted fraud detection, can deliver a return in months, while projects that require human involvement, such as AI-supported customer service, are likely to pay off over a longer period. Prioritization should be based on a long-term (typically three-year) view and take into consideration how several initiatives with different time lines could be combined to maximize value. For example, to achieve a view of customers detailed enough to allow AI to do microsegmentation, a company might need to set up a number of sales and marketing initiatives. Some, such as targeted offers, might deliver value in a few months, while it might take 12 to 18 months for the entire suite of capabilities to achieve full impact.

An Asian Pacific retailer determined that an AI initiative to optimize floor space and inventory placement wouldn't yield its complete value unless the company refurbished all its stores, reallocating the space for each category of goods. After much debate, the firm's executives decided the project was important enough to future profitability to proceed—but not without splitting it in two. Part one produced an AI tool that gave store managers recommendations for a few incremental items that would sell well in their outlets. The tool provided only a small fraction of the total return anticipated, but the managers could get the new items into stores immediately, demonstrating the project's benefits and building enthusiasm for the multiyear journey ahead.

Organizing for Scale

There's a lot of debate about where AI and analytics capabilities should reside within organizations. Often leaders simply ask, "What organizational model works best?" and then, after hearing what succeeded at other companies, do one of three things: consolidate the majority of AI and analytics capabilities within a central "hub"; decentralize them and embed them mostly in the business units ("the spokes"); or distribute them across both, using a hybrid ("hub-and-spoke") model. We've found that none of these models is always better than the others at getting AI up to scale; the right choice depends on a firm's individual situation.

Consider two large financial institutions we've worked with. One consolidated its AI and analytics teams in a central hub, with all analytics staff reporting to the chief data and analytics officer and being deployed to business units as needed. The second decentralized nearly all its analytics talent, having teams reside in and report to the business units. Both firms developed AI on a scale at the top of their industry; the second organization grew from 30 to 200 profitable AI initiatives in just two years. And both selected their model after taking into account their organizations' structure, capabilities, strategy, and unique characteristics.

The hub

A small handful of responsibilities are always best handled by a hub and led by the chief analytics or chief data officer. These include data governance, AI recruiting and training strategy, and work with third-party providers of data and AI services and software. Hubs should nurture AI talent, create communities where AI experts can share best practices, and lay out processes for AI development across the organization. Our research shows that companies that have implemented AI on a large scale are three times as likely as their peers to have a hub and 2.5 times as likely to have a clear methodology for creating models, interpreting insights, and deploying new AI capabilities.

Hubs should also be responsible for systems and standards related to AI. These should be driven by the needs of a firm's initiatives, which means they should be developed gradually, rather than set up in one fell swoop, before business cases have been determined. We've seen many organizations squander significant time and money—spending hundreds of millions of dollars—up front on companywide data-cleaning and data-integration projects, only to abort those efforts midway, realizing little or no benefits.

In contrast, when a European bank found that conflicting data-management strategies were hindering its development of new AI tools, it took a slower approach, making a plan to unify its data architecture and management over the next four years as it built various business cases for its AI transformation. This multiphase program, which also includes an organizational redesign and a revised talent strategy, is expected to have an annual impact of more than $900 million.

The spokes

Another handful of responsibilities should almost always be owned by the spokes, because they're closest to those who will be using the AI systems. Among them are tasks related to adoption, including end-user training, workflow redesign, incentive programs, performance management, and impact tracking.

To encourage customers to embrace the AI-enabled services offered with its smart, connected equipment, one manufacturer's sales and service organization created a "SWAT team" that supported customers using the product and developed a pricing plan to boost adoption. Such work is clearly the bailiwick of a spoke and can't be delegated to an analytics hub.

The gray area

Much of the work in successful AI transformations falls into a gray area in terms of responsibility. Key tasks—setting the direction for AI projects, analyzing the problems they'll solve, building the algorithms, designing the tools, testing them with end users, managing the change, and creating the supporting IT infrastructure—can be owned by either the hub or the spoke, shared by both, or shared with IT. (See the exhibit "Organizing AI for scale.") Deciding where

Organizing AI for scale

AI-enabled companies divide key roles between a hub and spokes. A few tasks are always owned by the hub, and the spokes always own execution. The rest of the work falls into a gray area, and a firm's individual characteristics determine where it should be done.

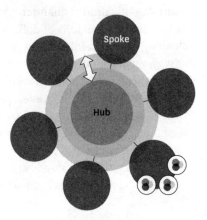

Governing coalition
A team of business, IT, and analytics leaders that share accountability for the AI transformation

 Hub
A central group headed by a C-level analytics executive who aligns strategy

Responsibilities
- Talent recruitment and training strategy
- Performance management
- Partnerships with providers of data and AI services and software
- AI standards, processes, policies

 Gray area
Work that could be owned by the hub or spokes or shared with IT

Responsibilities
- Project direction, delivery, change management
- Data strategy, data architecture, code development
- User experience
- IT infrastructure
- Organizational capability assessment, strategy, funding

 Spoke
A business unit, function, or geography, which assigns a manager to be the AI product owner and a business analyst to assist him or her

Responsibilities
- Oversight of execution teams
- Solution adoption
- Performance tracking

Execution teams
Assembled from the hub, spoke, and gray area for the duration of the project

Key roles
- Product owner
- Analytics translator
- Data scientist
- Data engineer
- Data architect
- Visualization specialist
- UI designer
- Business analyst

responsibility should lie within an organization is not an exact science, but it should be influenced by three factors:

The maturity of AI capabilities. When a company is early in its AI journey, it often makes sense for analytics executives, data scientists, data engineers, user interface designers, visualization specialists who graphically interpret analytics findings, and the like to sit within a hub and be deployed as needed to the spokes. Working together, these players can establish the company's core AI assets and capabilities, such as common analytics tools, data processes, and delivery methodologies. But as time passes and processes become standardized, these experts can reside within the spokes just as (or more) effectively.

Business model complexity. The greater the number of business functions, lines of business, or geographies AI tools will support, the greater the need to build guilds of AI experts (of, say, data scientists or designers). Companies with complex businesses often consolidate these guilds in the hub and then assign them out as needed to business units, functions, or geographies.

The pace and level of technical innovation required. When they need to innovate rapidly, some companies put more gray-area strategy and capability building in the hub so they can monitor industry and technology changes better and quickly deploy AI resources to head off competitive challenges.

Let's return to the two financial institutions we discussed earlier. Both faced competitive pressures that required rapid innovation. However, their analytics maturity and business complexity differed.

The institution that placed its analytics teams within its hub had a much more complex business model and relatively low AI maturity. Its existing AI expertise was primarily in risk management. By concentrating its data scientists, engineers, and many other gray-area experts within the hub, the company ensured that all business units and functions could rapidly access essential know-how when needed.

The second financial institution had a much simpler business model that involved specializing in fewer financial services. This bank also had substantial AI experience and expertise. So it was able to decentralize its AI talent, embedding many of its gray-area analytics, strategy, and technology experts within the business-unit spokes.

As these examples suggest, some art is involved in deciding where responsibilities should live. Every organization has distinctive capabilities and competitive pressures, and the three key factors must be considered in totality, rather than individually. For example, an organization might have high business complexity and need very rapid innovation (suggesting it should shift more responsibilities to the hub) but also have very mature AI capabilities (suggesting it should move them to the spokes). Its leaders would have to weigh the relative importance of all three factors to determine where, on balance, talent would most effectively be deployed. Talent levels (an element of AI maturity) often have an outsize influence on the decision. Does the organization have enough data experts that, if it moved them permanently to the spokes, it could still fill the needs of all business units, functions, and geographies? If not, it would probably be better to house them in the hub and share them throughout the organization.

Oversight and execution

While the distribution of AI and analytics responsibilities varies from one organization to the next, those that scale up AI have two things in common:

A governing coalition of business, IT, and analytics leaders. Fully integrating AI is a long journey. Creating a joint task force to oversee it will ensure that the three functions collaborate and share accountability, regardless of how roles and responsibilities are divided. This group, which is often convened by the chief analytics officer, can also be instrumental in building momentum for AI initiatives, especially early on.

Assignment-based execution teams. Organizations that scale up AI are twice as likely to set up interdisciplinary teams within the spokes. Such teams bring a diversity of perspectives together and solicit input from frontline staff as they build, deploy, and monitor new AI capabilities. The teams are usually assembled at the outset of each initiative and draw skills from both the hub and the spokes. Each generally includes the manager in charge of the new AI tool's success (the "product owner"), translators, data architects, engineers and scientists, designers, visualization specialists, and business analysts. These teams address implementation issues early and extract value faster.

For example, at the Asian Pacific retailer that was using AI to optimize store space and inventory placement, an interdisciplinary execution team helped break down walls between merchandisers (who determined how items would be displayed in stores) and buyers (who chose the range of products). Previously, each group had worked independently, with the buyers altering the AI recommendations as they saw fit. That led to a mismatch between inventory purchased and space available. By inviting both groups to collaborate on the further development of the AI tool, the team created a more effective model that provided a range of weighted options to the buyers, who could then choose the best ones with input from the merchandisers. At the end of the process, gross margins on each product category that had applied the tool increased by 4% to 7%.

Educating Everyone

To ensure the adoption of AI, companies need to educate everyone, from the top leaders down. To this end some are launching internal AI academies, which typically incorporate classroom work (online or in person), workshops, on-the-job training, and even site visits to experienced industry peers. Most academies initially hire external faculty to write the curricula and deliver training, but they also usually put in place processes to build in-house capabilities.

Every academy is different, but most offer four broad types of instruction:

Leadership
Most academies strive to give senior executives and business-unit leaders a high-level understanding of how AI works and ways to

10 Ways to Derail an AI Program

DESPITE BIG INVESTMENTS, many organizations get disappointing results from their AI and analytics efforts. What makes programs go off track? Companies set themselves up to fail when:

1. They lack a clear understanding of advanced analytics, staffing up with data scientists, engineers, and other key players without realizing how advanced and traditional analytics differ.

2. They don't assess feasibility, business value, and time horizons, and launch pilots without thinking through how to balance short-term wins in the first year with longer-term payoffs.

3. They have no strategy beyond a few use cases, tackling AI in an ad hoc way without considering the big-picture opportunities and threats AI presents in their industry.

4. They don't clearly define key roles, because they don't understand the tapestry of skill sets and tasks that a strong AI program requires.

5. They lack "translators," or experts who can bridge the business and analytics realms by identifying high-value use cases, communicating business needs to tech experts, and generating buy-in with business users.

6. They isolate analytics from the business, rigidly centralizing it or locking it in poorly coordinated silos, rather than organizing it in ways that allow analytics and business experts to work closely together.

7. They squander time and money on enterprisewide data cleaning instead of aligning data consolidation and cleanup with their most valuable use cases.

8. They fully build out analytics platforms before identifying business cases, setting up architectures like data lakes without knowing what they'll be needed for and often integrating platforms with legacy systems unnecessarily.

9. They neglect to quantify analytics' bottom-line impact, lacking a performance management framework with clear metrics for tracking each initiative.

10. They fail to focus on ethical, social, and regulatory implications, leaving themselves vulnerable to potential missteps when it comes to data acquisition and use, algorithmic bias, and other risks, and exposing themselves to social and legal consequences.

For more details, read "Ten Red Flags Signaling Your Analytics Program Will Fail" on McKinsey.com.

identify and prioritize AI opportunities. They also provide discussions of the impact on workers' roles, barriers to adoption, and talent development, and offer guidance on instilling the underlying cultural changes required.

Analytics

Here the focus is on constantly sharpening the hard and soft skills of data scientists, engineers, architects, and other employees who are responsible for data analytics, data governance, and building the AI solutions.

Translator

Analytics translators often come from the business staff and need fundamental technical training—for instance, in how to apply analytical approaches to business problems and develop AI use cases. Their instruction may include online tutorials, hands-on experience shadowing veteran translators, and a final "exam" in which they must successfully implement an AI initiative.

End user

Frontline workers may need only a general introduction to new AI tools, followed by on-the-job training and coaching in how to use them. Strategic decision makers, such as marketers and finance staff, may require higher-level training sessions that incorporate real business scenarios in which new tools improve decisions about, say, product launches.

Reinforcing the Change

Most AI transformations take 18 to 36 months to complete, with some taking as long as five years. To prevent them from losing momentum, leaders need to do four things:

Walk the talk

Role modeling is essential. For starters, leaders can demonstrate their commitment to AI by attending academy training.

But they also must actively encourage new ways of working. AI requires experimentation, and often early iterations don't work out as planned. When that happens, leaders should highlight what was learned from the pilots. That will help encourage appropriate risk taking.

The most effective role models we've seen are humble. They ask questions and reinforce the value of diverse perspectives. They regularly meet with staff to discuss the data, asking questions such as "How often are we right?" and "What data do we have to support today's decision?"

The CEO of one specialty retailer we know is a good example. At every meeting she goes to, she invites attendees to share their experience and opinions—and offers hers last. She also makes time to meet with business and analytics employees every few weeks to see what they've done—whether it's launching a new pilot or scaling up an existing one.

Make businesses accountable

It's not uncommon to see analytics staff made the owners of AI products. However, because analytics are simply a means of solving business problems, it's the business units that must lead projects and be responsible for their success. Ownership ought to be assigned to someone from the relevant business, who should map out roles and guide a project from start to finish. Sometimes organizations assign different owners at different points in the development life cycle (for instance, for proof of value, deployment, and scaling). That's a mistake too, because it can result in loose ends or missed opportunities.

A scorecard that captures project performance metrics for all stakeholders is an excellent way to align the goals of analytics and business teams. One airline company, for instance, used a shared scorecard to measure rate of adoption, speed to full capability, and business outcomes for an AI solution that optimized pricing and booking.

Track and facilitate adoption

Comparing the results of decisions made with and without AI can encourage employees to use it. For example, at one commodity company, traders learned that their non-AI-supported forecasts were typically right only half the time—no better than guessing. That discovery made them more open to AI tools for improved forecasting. Teams that monitor implementation can correct course as needed. At one North American retailer, an AI project owner saw store managers struggling to incorporate a pilot's output into their tracking of store performance results. The AI's user interface was difficult to navigate, and the AI insights generated weren't integrated into the dashboards the managers relied on every day to make decisions. To fix the issue, the AI team simplified the interface and reconfigured the output so that the new data stream appeared in the dashboard.

Provide incentives for change

Acknowledgment inspires employees for the long haul. The CEO of the specialty retailer starts meetings by shining a spotlight on an employee (such as a product manager, a data scientist, or a frontline worker) who has helped make the company's AI program a success. At the large retail conglomerate, the CEO created new roles for top performers who participated in the AI transformation. For instance, he promoted the category manager who helped test the optimization solution during its pilot to lead its rollout across stores—visibly demonstrating the career impact that embracing AI could have.

Finally, firms have to check that employees' incentives are truly aligned with AI use. This was not the case at a brick-and-mortar retailer that had developed an AI model to optimize discount pricing so that it could clear out old stock. The model revealed that sometimes it was more profitable to dispose of old stock than to sell it at a discount, but the store personnel had incentives to sell everything, even at steep discounts. Because the AI recommendations contradicted their standard, rewarded practice, employees became suspicious of the tool and ignored it. Since their sales incentives were also closely tied to contracts and couldn't easily be changed, the organization ultimately updated the AI model to recognize the trade-off between profits and the incentives, which helped drive user adoption and lifted the bottom line.

The actions that promote scale in AI create a virtuous circle. The move from functional to interdisciplinary teams initially brings together the diverse skills and perspectives and the user input needed to build effective tools. In time, workers across the organization absorb new collaborative practices. As they work more closely with colleagues in other functions and geographies, employees begin to think bigger—they move from trying to solve discrete problems to completely reimagining business and operating models. The speed of innovation picks up as the rest of the organization begins to adopt the test-and-learn approaches that successfully propelled the pilots.

As AI tools spread throughout the organization, those closest to the action become increasingly able to make decisions once made by those above them, flattening organizational hierarchies. That encourages further collaboration and even bigger thinking.

The ways AI can be used to augment decision making keep expanding. New applications will create fundamental and sometimes difficult changes in workflows, roles, and culture, which leaders will need to shepherd their organizations through carefully. Companies that excel at implementing AI throughout the organization will find themselves at a great advantage in a world where humans and machines working together outperform either humans or machines working on their own.

Originally published in July–August 2019. Reprint R1904C

Leading a New Era of Climate Action

by Andrew Winston

CLIMATE CHANGE IS A GLOBAL EMERGENCY. It's threatening crops, water supplies, infrastructure, and livelihoods. It's damaging the broader economy and company bottom lines *today*, not in some distant future. In recent years AT&T has spent $874 million on repairs after natural disasters that the company ties to climate change. The reinsurance leader Swiss Re has seen large increases in payouts for damage caused by extreme weather events—$2.5 billion more in 2017 than it had predicted—a trend that CEO Christian Mumenthaler attributes to rising global temperatures. If we don't move quickly toward action on climate, says Mark Carney, the Bank of England governor, we'll see company bankruptcies and raise the odds of systemic economic collapse.

Corporate leaders are at last absorbing this; nearly every large company has significant plans to cut carbon emissions and is acting. But given the scale of the crisis and the pace at which it's developing, these efforts are woefully inadequate. Critical UN reports in 2018 and 2019 make two things clear: (1) To avoid *some* of the worst outcomes of climate change, the world must cut carbon emissions by 45% by 2030 and eliminate them entirely by midcentury. (2) Current government plans and commitments are not remotely close to putting us on that path. Emissions are still rising.

Countries, cities, and businesses need to move simultaneously along two paths: reducing emissions dramatically (mitigation) and investing in resilience while planning for vast change (adaptation). My focus here is on mitigation, because adaptation alone—building ever-higher walls to keep out the sea and simply turning up the air-conditioning as the outdoors becomes uninhabitable—won't save us. If we allow climate change to destroy the plant and animal ecosystems we rely on, there will be no replacements. The good news is that business has enormous potential to profitably cut emissions faster and even more.

If the main question for business were still "Which actions will both cut emissions and create short-term value?" we know the answer: slash carbon in energy-intensive industries and in operations, transportation, and buildings; buy lots of renewable energy, which is strategically smart because it has been competitive with fossil fuels for years; reduce waste, particularly in critical sectors such as food and agriculture; expand the use of circular business models that minimize resource use; embed climate change metrics in corporate systems and key performance indicators; and more. Again, most companies have begun to take advantage of these "basic" opportunities and will accelerate adoption as they see the payoff grow. So let's assume that they will continue down this path. Then what?

Given the urgency, we must ask a different, and harder, question: "What are *all* the things business can possibly do with its vast resources?" What capital—financial, human, brand, and political—can companies bring to bear?

Drawing on 20 years of consulting to global corporations and working on climate change issues, I see three actions that companies must now focus on to drive deeper change:

- using political influence to demand aggressive climate policies around the world
- empowering suppliers, customers, and employees to drive change
- rethinking investments and business models to eliminate waste and carbon throughout the economy

Idea in Brief

Climate change is a global emergency that threatens crops, water supplies, infrastructure, and livelihoods. It's damaging the economy and company bottom lines. Most large companies are cutting carbon emissions, but given the scale of the crisis, these efforts are sadly inadequate. Companies need to mobilize, says Andrew Winston, to deal with this unprecedented global problem. He draws on 20 years of consulting for global corporations to recommend three actions:

- Use political influence to demand aggressive climate policies.

- Empower suppliers, customers, and employees to drive change.

- Rethink investments and business models to eliminate waste and carbon.

These actions may feel unnatural to some executives if they appear to put larger interests ahead of immediate shareholder profits. But the tide is turning on the very idea of shareholder primacy. The roughly 200 largest multinationals based in the United States recently declared, through the Business Roundtable, that they will no longer focus solely on shareholders or on the short run. We are at a pivotal moment as the climate crisis propels companies' growing sense of social purpose. The result, I believe, is the will needed to finally achieve this deeper change.

What's in It for Us?

Before I dig into the three areas of change, it's fair to ask why a company would commit to such challenging and possibly risky initiatives. One argument is macro/societal and the other is microeconomic. The former is straightforward: Companies need healthy people and a viable planet; with expensive runaway climate change on the horizon, they have an economic imperative and a moral responsibility to do everything they can to ensure a thriving world. As Unilever's former CEO Paul Polman says, "Business simply can't be a bystander in a system that gives it life in the first place." And let's not forget that even as they pursue their own self-interest, executives sometimes just do what they believe is the right thing,

The Big Idea: Mobilizing on Climate

"Leading a New Era of Climate Action" is the lead article of HBR's **The Big Idea: Mobilizing on Climate.** Read the rest of the series at hbr.org/climate:

- "Tough Business Questions about the Climate Crisis," by Andy Robinson
- "What Do People Really Believe about Climate Change?" by Gretchen Gavett
- "Your Company's Next Leader on Climate Is . . . the CFO," by Laura Palmeiro and Delphine Gibassier
- "The New Business of Garbage," by Laura Amico
- "A Better Way to Talk about the Climate Crisis," by Gretchen Gavett
- "Is Your Trade Group Blocking Climate Action?" by Sheldon Whitehouse

which may or may not pay off—from ceasing to sell assault weapons at Dick's Sporting Goods and Walmart to funding by Apple and Microsoft of programs to reduce homelessness in their neighborhoods.

The microeconomic argument, however, is often overlooked. Stakeholders, particularly customers and employees, have increasingly high standards for the companies they buy from and work for. Business customers are demanding more sustainability performance from suppliers every year. Consumers are seeking out sustainable brands (50% of consumer packaged goods growth from 2013 to 2018 came from sustainability-marketed products), and Deloitte's global surveys show that up to 87% of the under-40 crowd—the Millennials who will make up 75% of the global workforce in five years—believes that a company's success should be measured in more than just financial terms. And nine in 10 members of Gen Z agree that companies have a responsibility to engage with environmental and social issues.

Employees are now directly pressuring their companies to do more on climate, particularly in the tech sector. In direct and public appeals, Google employees have asked their executives to cut ties to climate deniers, and Microsoft's employees staged a walkout in protest of the company's "complicity in the climate crisis." At Amazon more than 8,700 workers have signed an open letter to CEO Jeff

Alarming forecast: current climate policies are grossly inadequate

To hold global warming to 1.5° Celsius above preindustrial levels and prevent the worst impacts of climate change, the world must cut carbon emissions to zero by midcentury. Yet emissions are still rising, and under existing policies reductions won't begin to approach what's needed. If we stay on the current path, temperatures will probably increase by about 3° C, with catastrophic effects.

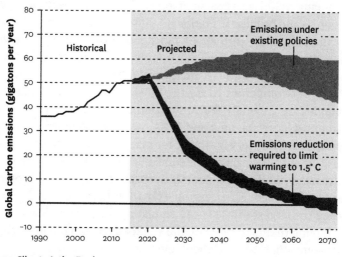

Source: Climate Action Tracker.

Note: Bandwidths represent high and low emissions estimates.

Bezos with a list of demands, including developing a plan to get to zero emissions and eliminating donations to climate-denying legislators. Their efforts clearly played a part in pushing Bezos to announce large ambitions to be carbon neutral by 2040 and to buy 100,000 electric vehicles.

Because of pressure like this, along with increasingly dire warnings from climate scientists and global bodies including the UN, corporate efforts to reduce emissions have become table stakes— something any company *must* do to earn respect from employees and customers. And what is common and accepted practice, regardless of the short-term ROI, can sometimes shift very quickly. Consider that nobody could prove the value of diversity and inclusion when companies first dove into that issue. Now we have good data—but the norms changed first.

I've seen firsthand how this can play out on sustainability issues. Nearly six years ago, in my book *The Big Pivot*, I advocated setting science-based emissions-reduction goals. Virtually no companies were doing that then, and I argued with many who wondered why a company would set a goal not required by law. Now, owing to peer pressure—and because it's rational—those goals are all but standard for big companies, with about 750 signed up and more than 200 committing to 100% renewable energy. They moved from "Why would we?" to "You're a laggard if you don't."

The first companies to try the most innovative sustainability strategies are generally B Corps or purpose-driven, privately held businesses like Patagonia and IKEA, which have more leeway to experiment. The story is similar for many of the next-gen climate ideas I lay out below: Big public companies are just dipping their toes in the water, while smaller, nimbler, sustainability-focused companies take the lead. Their examples matter, because over the past decade the largest firms started emulating the midsize leaders—or just buying them. To mitigate the worst effects of climate change, more companies need to follow, and fast.

Let's return now to the three broad activities that every company, big or small, must undertake.

1. Use Political Influence for Climate Good

Given the scale of the climate crisis, business alone can't solve it. But business does have a powerful tool beyond its own practices and products: extensive and deep tendrils in the halls of political power. All over the world, but especially in market economies, companies have enormous influence over governments and politicians. Through large campaign donations and—in the United States after the Supreme Court case *Citizens United*—nearly unlimited spending on political ads, the corporate agenda gets an outsize voice in society. How can and should companies use that power?

Business's government relations have traditionally been aimed at reshaping or fighting regulations. But over the past few years many companies have, at least on the surface, been supporting some climate policy. Hundreds of multinationals with operations in the U.S. have signed statements such as "We Are Still In" and the recent "United for the Paris Agreement" to let the world know that they will cut emissions in keeping with the Paris Climate Accords and that they want the U.S. government to stay aboard, despite announcements that it would not. Another group of large companies called for the world to hold warming to just 1.5 degrees Celsius. Signatories came from every corner of the planet: Sweden (Electrolux), Japan (ASICS), India (Mahindra Group), Switzerland (Nestlé), Germany (SAP), and many other places and sectors.

But statements alone are inadequate. Companies must lobby for the policies that will lead to a low-carbon future, and senior executives need to show up in person. Without collective government action, we have little chance of avoiding the direst outcomes of climate change. One industry—fossil fuels—has had a dominant, decades-long influence on climate policies in world capitals, and for good reason: Policies aimed at reducing emissions pose an existential threat to the business. Companies in every other sector must grasp that climate change, which may spin out of control without enlightened policies, is an existential threat to *their* businesses.

For the most part, nonfossil fuel companies engage only in occasional special lobbying days organized by the likes of Ceres, the American Sustainable Business Council, and Business Climate Leaders. Those events are important, of course, but even the groups themselves acknowledge that the number of big companies with a consistent climate-action focus is small. As Joe Britton, a former chief of staff for U.S. senator Martin Heinrich, told me, these temporary "fly-ins" are better than nothing, but they are overshadowed by the daily swarm of fossil fuel lobbyists. In response, Britton left his position to create a new lobbying organization, with the help of other Capitol Hill insiders, to deploy a fuller and more constant political message to Congress on climate.

There's also a major disconnect between what companies say about their commitments to fight climate change and what those who represent them—the trade associations or even their own government relations people—actually push for. As transparency increases, companies should worry about any gap between their sustainability commitments and their lobbying. An NGO, Australia's LobbyWatch, is calling out the mining giant BHP and others for such disconnects. And the UK-based influencemap.org is tracking corporate lobbying activity on climate at hundreds of companies and publicly highlighting hypocrisy.

For leaders, aggressive climate lobbying is not just about appearances; it can create advantage. If 100% of your energy comes from renewables, a price on carbon won't affect your own cost structure much. And if you make products or provide services that help reduce emissions, you benefit from tighter carbon controls. That's surely one reason that Germany's Siemens, with a portfolio of products that improve energy efficiency, states that its top political engagement goal is "combating Climate Change."

Hugh Welsh, the president for North America at DSM, a large Dutch company that offers nutrition, health, and sustainable-living products and solutions, can attest to this. He has worked for years to bring a business voice on climate to the halls of political power. Welsh says he does this for two reasons: principles and pragmatism. About the former, he says, "Over 10 years as president, I've developed political capital. I can use that just for strategic things for the business, but I can also use that to improve the world." About the latter, he notes that DSM serves several sustainability-focused product markets, so a proactive role on sustainability and climate policy fits its strategy.

When Welsh makes the case to skeptical executives, leaders, and trade groups—such as the recalcitrant U.S. Chamber of Commerce, with which he worked for two years to flip its position on climate—he says, "If you don't evolve your position, you'll be on the wrong side of history . . . your partners and customers will leave in droves."

Rising temperatures, rising risks: flooding cities

If the global temperature were to increase by . . .

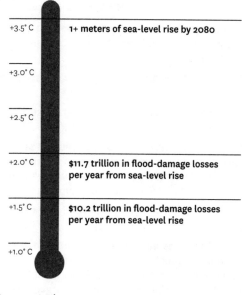

+3.5° C	1+ meters of sea-level rise by 2080
+3.0° C	
+2.5° C	
+2.0° C	$11.7 trillion in flood-damage losses per year from sea-level rise
+1.5° C	$10.2 trillion in flood-damage losses per year from sea-level rise
+1.0° C	

Source: World Resources Institute.

So what policies should companies advocate? To move the world to a low-carbon future, we need bold plans in a few key areas: pricing carbon and mobilizing capital to shift to low-carbon systems; rapidly raising performance standards and phasing out old technologies for big energy users like cars and buildings; and enabling transparency and efforts to reduce human suffering.

These priorities apply in most geographies, but of course policy formation and the relationship between business and government vary widely across countries. Approaches in command-and-control economies must vary from those in sprawling capitalist systems.

Policies may take years to have an effect, so these efforts must be made soon. It's time for companies to use their substantial political

Climate Policies Companies Should Fight For

A long list of possible government policies could create the conditions for rapid emissions reductions. But the following are probably the most important for business to get behind. These will fix market failures, shift capital toward low-carbon investments, and set a high bar for low-carbon products.

Implement a rapidly rising price on carbon, coupled with massive shifts in subsidies from fossil fuels to clean tech and low-carbon production methods.

Create incentives for farmers to move from industrial to regenerative agriculture.

Fund increased material capture (recycling, reuse, repair) to encourage a circular economy.

Mobilize capital and R&D that pulls public and private investment into cleaner tech. For example, the Danish aviation sector has proposed a climate tax on all flights from Denmark, earmarked for a fund to research green solutions and climate-neutral fuels.

Introduce high performance standards for the big energy users, including cars, buildings, and HVAC systems.

Encourage phaseouts and phase-ins such as by mandating low-global-warming-potential refrigerants and net-zero buildings with renewables and banning gas-guzzlers. Some countries have set a date for stopping the sale of internal combustion engines: Norway by 2025, Sweden and Denmark by 2030, and France and Sri Lanka by 2040.

Prioritize transparency through, for example, the Task Force on Climate-related Financial Disclosures, which provides guidelines for companies reporting their material risks from climate change, and product labels with carbon-footprint information, much like the calorie and nutrition counts on food labels.

Fund resources for adaptation, such as resilience planning in cities, the relocation of citizens, and retraining for those from older sectors that will rapidly decline.

influence to proactively support laws that make high-carbon products and choices more expensive, mobilize capital toward a clean economy, support systems change, and help deal with adaptation and the human costs of shifts to clean technology.

2. Leverage Stakeholder Relationships

At the same time, companies should wield their other superpower: vast influence over value chain partners and deep connections to their customers and employees. Big consumer products companies like P&G and Unilever often rightly brag that they serve billions of people every day. More than 275 million people visit a Walmart every week. Companies employ hundreds of millions of us. And with nearly $33 trillion in revenues across the *Fortune* Global 500 alone, it's safe to assume that many trillions go to suppliers. Imagine if companies used those touch points, their buying power, and all their communications and advertising clout to catalyze change across business and society.

Suppliers

In recent years corporations have ratcheted up the pressure on their suppliers to operate more sustainably. Big buyers increasingly want to see progress—backed up by data—in a supplier's carbon footprint, resource use, human rights and labor performance, and much more. General Mills, Kellogg, IKEA, and Hewlett Packard Enterprise have all set science-based carbon goals for their suppliers. Others, including GSK, H&M, Toyota, and Schneider Electric, have committed to carbon neutrality or negativity (eliminating more carbon than is produced) in their entire value chains by 2040 or 2050.

Commitments like these are becoming the norm. But what else is possible? What are boundary-pushing companies doing to drive change? I see future supply-chain climate leadership in three key areas: providing capital, driving innovation and collaboration, and using purchasing power to choose suppliers on the basis of emissions performance.

Financial assistance and capital. Making a business more sustainable is profitable, but it may still require investments and capital. Companies that ask suppliers to change how they do business can help, especially with smaller players. For example, in mid-2018, after achieving 100% renewable energy in its own operations, Apple launched the China Clean Energy Fund, a joint pool of $300 million

Rising temperatures, rising risks: food shortages

If the global temperature were to increase by . . .

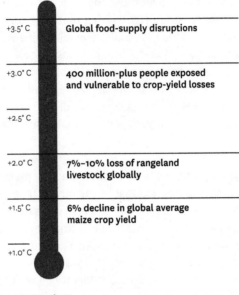

+3.5° C	Global food-supply disruptions
+3.0° C	400 million-plus people exposed and vulnerable to crop-yield losses
+2.5° C	
+2.0° C	7%–10% loss of rangeland livestock globally
+1.5° C	6% decline in global average maize crop yield
+1.0° C	

Source: World Resources Institute.

to help suppliers buy one gigawatt of renewable energy, and the fund's first big wind farms went up last year. Similarly, IKEA recently committed €100 million to help first-tier suppliers make the shift. In another innovative approach, an industrial company I work with, Ingersoll Rand (better known by its brands Thermo King and Trane), financed a large renewable energy project and then invited suppliers to offset their emissions by buying portions of the energy production. And beyond encouraging renewables, some leaders, such as Levi's and Walmart, have worked with HSBC and other banks to provide lower interest rates to suppliers that score well on sustainability performance.

Joint innovation. I also recently watched the head of procurement at Ingersoll Rand tell hundreds of suppliers that his company would no longer choose vendors on the basis of pricing and quality alone. Now, he said, suppliers would need to innovate *with* the company to make its products more energy- and carbon-efficient. This is a great way to drive value chain innovation, but sectorwide collaboration can have an even bigger impact.

Consider that Walmart and Target, which are traditionally competitors, worked together with the NGO Forum for the Future (on whose board I serve) to create the Beauty and Personal Care Sustainability Project—a creative attempt at improving the environmental and social footprint of all the products we put on our bodies. They brought together big CPG companies such as P&G and Unilever and their chemical suppliers to rethink ingredients, packaging, and more to reduce health and environmental impacts. Apple has dived deep into its supply chain to make its ubiquitous tech products lower-carbon, including through a joint venture with Rio Tinto and Alcoa to develop and commercialize an aluminum-smelting process with vastly lower greenhouse gas emissions and lower costs.

Purchasing power. For years many companies have agreed to work with lagging suppliers to improve their sustainability performance. But the world can no longer afford to wait for slow adopters. Companies should cut them loose and shift their purchasing dollars toward the low-carbon leaders—which are often the best-run suppliers anyway. VF Corporation, the home of brands such as Vans and The North Face, stopped buying leather from Brazil because government policy there was encouraging Amazon rain forest destruction.

Retailers should make carbon performance a buying priority. Mainstream mega-retailers like Walmart and Target have pressured suppliers for years to make their offerings more sustainable, but they could do much more to support those that are best at reducing emissions in their operations or through their products. They could, for example, permanently (not just on Earth Day) devote endcaps or special promotion areas—their highest-value real estate—to drive business to the lowest-carbon-emitting suppliers while satisfying growing customer demand for green products. It's a win-win, but it's not normal practice yet.

Customers

The core thing companies are doing—and must continue to do—is helping customers reduce carbon emissions by developing and offering products that produce fewer emissions throughout their life cycles. We're seeing great innovation, and customer buy-in, for lower-footprint products in the biggest carbon-emitting sectors: electric vehicles in transportation; efficient heating, cooling, and lighting in buildings; and tasty alternative proteins in food and agriculture.

Manufacturers and retailers are also working to increase the use of recycled materials and reduce the amount of material used in packaging—all the way to zero in some cases. A group of British retailers, for example, has teamed up to change how some products leave the store. Consumers can fill their own bags and jars from bins of dry goods (grains, beans, nuts, and so on), laundry detergent, and shampoo. Some commercial products are trying to go even further: After making each tile of its prototype carbon-negative flooring, Interface explains, "there is less carbon dioxide in the atmosphere than if it had not been manufactured in the first place."

But businesses need to make products like these mainstream and then go beyond the direct impacts of their products on customers to drive deeper change. Here are three possible ways forward:

Help customers use less and mobilize. The two most aggressive actions companies can take with consumers are encouraging them to reduce consumption and engaging them in climate activism. Zurich-based Freitag, which makes bags from recycled materials, lets customers create a new look by switching bags with other customers. And Patagonia (always a radical company) is teaching its customers how to repair its clothes so that they don't need to buy new items. These companies may risk selling less, but they're building trusted brands with a loyal following. And discouraging consumption hasn't hurt Patagonia in the least: Sales have quadrupled

Rising temperatures, rising risks: nature's collapse
If the global temperature were to increase by . . .

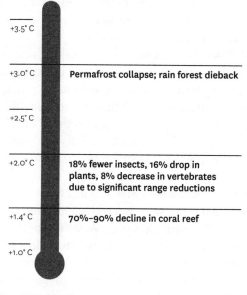

+3.5° C

+3.0° C   Permafrost collapse; rain forest dieback

+2.5° C

+2.0° C   18% fewer insects, 16% drop in plants, 8% decrease in vertebrates due to significant range reductions

+1.4° C   70%–90% decline in coral reef

+1.0° C

Source: World Resources Institute.

over the past decade, reaching an estimated $1 billion. Going further, the company is using the trust it has built to mobilize consumers, through its Patagonia Action Works initiative, to engage with grassroots environmental groups in Europe and the United States.

Use communications to educate and inspire consumers. Companies can make more-effective use of two channels in driving climate discussions: packaging and advertising. How? The Swedish oat drink brand Oatly, for example, reports product carbon emissions on its packages and points consumers to information on the climate benefits of eating plant-based products. Ben & Jerry's used the packaging and launch of an ice cream flavor, Save Our Swirled, to raise awareness about the Paris Climate Accords in 2015. IKEA surveyed more than 14,000 customers in 14 countries to understand their attitudes and how best to motivate climate action through advertising; the resulting framework is designed to guide its communications. In the fall of 2019 the household products company Seventh Generation donated advertising airtime on the *Today* show to help promote the Youth Climate Movement.

A new collaborative initiative seeks to make promotional activities like these the norm. Launched recently by Sustainable Brands (on whose advisory board I sit)—along with some big names such as PepsiCo, Nestlé Waters, P&G, SC Johnson, and Visa—the Brands for Good program commits participants to encourage sustainable living through their marketing and communications and, even more ambitious, to transform the field of marketing to support that goal.

Choose business customers wisely. The efforts described above focus on traditional consumers. But companies need to direct equal attention to their business customers. As with suppliers, they must stop enabling customers that are either not addressing climate change or, more to the point, part of the high-carbon economy. Banks, venture capital and private equity funds, consulting companies, legal firms, and other service providers should ask tough questions about whom they're supporting. Helping companies be "better" at extracting or burning carbon-based fuels is actively moving the world in the wrong direction, and it dwarfs any carbon reduction a service business pursues in its own operations.

In the investment world, a movement to divest from fossil fuels is taking off, spearheaded by a group of investors with $11 trillion in assets. Norway's $1 trillion sovereign wealth fund is likewise dumping investments in many oil and gas companies.

Other service companies, such as consulting giants and law firms, that still work with carbon-intensive industries should be helping them make the permanent pivot necessary to survive. That means helping fossil fuel companies sunset their core business over the next few decades and completely shift their portfolios and business models toward clean options. Tech companies have to do some hard thinking as well. One of the reasons Amazon's employees rebelled was the company's announcement that its cloud business would help oil and gas companies accelerate exploration. Stakeholders will continue to ask probing questions about what companies stand for and whom they support—and companies will have to have an answer.

Employees

In the battle for talent, especially for Millennials and Gen Z, companies must prove that they are good citizens. Surveys consistently show that people under 40 want to work for employers that share their values. As Unilever's sustainable living plan gained steam in the mid-2010s, the company became the most sought-after employer in its sector. Top executives I've worked with at Unilever cite its sustainability leadership as key in attracting and retaining talent. The benefit flows both ways: Companies need their employees' commitment and buy-in to achieve their sustainability goals.

To reinforce this relationship, companies must build sustainability and climate action into their regular incentive structures and systems—that is, pay everyone from the C-suite on down to cut carbon. They are secretive about the exact percentages, but the most committed companies I've seen tie at least a quarter of bonuses to sustainability key performance indicators (KPIs). It's time to increase that.

Can companies go even further and proactively support their employees' values by helping them drive change in the world around them? Some organizations already do. During the 2018 U.S. election, more than 100 of them, including Walmart, Levi Strauss, The Gap, Southwest Airlines, Kaiser Permanente, and Lyft, joined the Time to Vote initiative, giving employees time off to be good citizens. Some even encourage direct climate activism. Having identified the "climate emergency" as a top employee concern, the $1 billion cosmetics retailer Lush closed 200 shops in the U.S. to allow employees to join global climate marches last September. A Lush representative told me that during Canadian marches the company also shuttered 50 shops and offices for 20 manufacturing and support teams.

Atlassian, the fast-growing Australian enterprise software company with a $30 billion market cap, also encourages employees to become climate activists. As the company's cofounder Mike Cannon-Brookes wrote in his blunt blog "Don't @#$% the planet," Atlassian gives employees a week each year to volunteer for charity, and they can now use the time to join marches and strikes. He wants them to "go further and volunteer their time to other not-for-profit groups with a focus on climate."

Employees want to work for a company that stands for something. But they increasingly also want the freedom to express what *they* stand for. So ask them what they care about—especially younger and newer employees—and help them live their values.

3. Rethinking the Business

Flexing political muscle and reconceiving stakeholder relationships must happen quickly. But it is also time to think big, to look for new possibilities, and to question core assumptions about consumption and growth in the economy—that is, to go far beyond simply slashing energy use and buying renewables. Today the possibilities are broad, with everything from reducing food waste to developing circular business models falling under the umbrella of "climate strategy." Now is the right time to think critically and creatively about how *all* products and services in every sector are created and used and to squeeze carbon out of every step in the value chain. Some of this is tactical—for example, working with suppliers or customers to reduce their emissions, as discussed. But at the strategic level it can mean rethinking the company's investments and business models entirely. Here are some ways to do just that, focused on two key areas.

Risk and investments

Companies deploy capital and make investment decisions in multiple ways. With some important changes in how they think about financing and investment, much more capital could flow to low-carbon activities.

Rising temperatures, rising risks: heat waves
If the global temperature were to increase by . . .

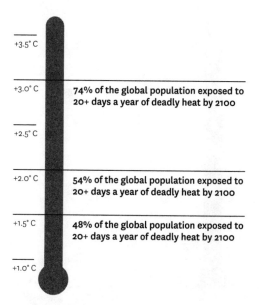

+3.5° C

+3.0° C — **74% of the global population exposed to 20+ days a year of deadly heat by 2100**

+2.5° C

+2.0° C — **54% of the global population exposed to 20+ days a year of deadly heat by 2100**

+1.5° C — **48% of the global population exposed to 20+ days a year of deadly heat by 2100**

+1.0° C

Source: World Resources Institute.

Note: According to research published in *Nature Climate Change*, "deadly heat" is the threshold beyond which air temperatures, humidity, and other factors can be lethal.

Consider the idea of return on investment. In most companies, to get internal funding, a project must achieve a predetermined rate of return (or hurdle rate) that will pay off relatively quickly. This approach to ROI is flawed. It generally measures the "R" in straight cash, without allowing for more-strategic or intangible value. It's also agnostic as to whether the investment moves the company down a more sustainable path. We need to use this tool differently to shift to low-carbon investment choices.

Smart tweaks to two internal processes—capital expenditures and hurdle rates—can do a lot of good. J.M. Huber, a family-owned

---

Rising temperatures, rising risks: water uncertainty

If the global temperature were to increase by . . .

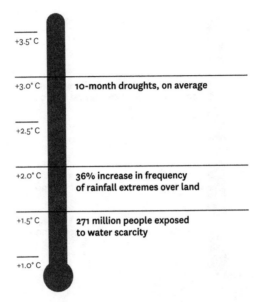

+3.5° C

+3.0° C — 10-month droughts, on average

+2.5° C

+2.0° C — 36% increase in frequency of rainfall extremes over land

+1.5° C — 271 million people exposed to water scarcity

+1.0° C

Source: World Resources Institute.

Note: According to the NOAA, "extreme rainfall" can be loosely defined as a month's worth of rain for a given region falling in a single day.

---

business that manufactures nature-based ingredients for the food and personal care industries along with components in home building, developed a more holistic approach to optimizing capital deployment. The chief sustainability officer and the CFO worked together to shift the capex process to factor in intangible benefits such as community engagement, customer perceptions, employee attraction and retention, and business resiliency (for example, solar array projects that insulate the business from fossil fuel energy price shocks).

Companies should set their hurdle rates more strategically and allow some investments more leeway, with a strong bias toward funding carbon-reducing projects. If, for example, constructing an energy-efficient building—one that will save money and carbon over its lifetime—costs more up front or requires more than a few years to pay off, isn't it still a smart investment on a 40-year asset?

Another wise investment shift involves levying an internal carbon price on companies' own operations to encourage emissions reduction. More than 1,400 organizations now use internal pricing in some way, but the norm is to use "shadow" prices with no money changing hands. That approach isn't strong enough. Early leaders like Microsoft, Disney, and LVMH have been collecting *real* money from divisions or functions related to their emissions. That "tax" revenue is reinvested in energy efficiency, renewables, or offset projects such as tree planting. All companies should use this strategy to help fund low-carbon projects and to prepare the business as government-imposed carbon taxes become more common.

A more recent strategy is to use financing tools such as green bonds, now a $200 billion market, in which the proceeds from bond purchases go to environmental and climate projects. The Italian energy group ENEL is trying something a bit different, issuing a bond tied to a KPI measuring the company's performance against the UN's Sustainable Development Goals. If ENEL misses its target of increasing renewable energy to 55% of its installed capacity, it will pay 25 basis points more to bondholders. Although the funds raised are not tied to a specific use, as they are with conventional green bonds, the instrument clearly supports emissions reduction.

Perhaps the biggest move a company can make is to rethink where to place its R&D bets. In a telling seismic shift, Daimler announced that it would no longer invest in research on internal combustion engines and would put billions toward electric vehicles instead. And the CEO of Nestlé, Mark Schneider, spoke recently about investing in plant-based proteins, which have a *much* smaller carbon footprint than conventionally produced meat, saying, "A Swiss franc we spend developing the burger is a burden to this quarter's profits. Next year or the year after, it will come back to us if we do our job right." Seeing returns on a fast-growing new market within a year or two sounds like a good deal.

New business models

The level of carbon reduction that the Intergovernmental Panel on Climate Change says is required to head off catastrophic warming—cutting emissions in half by 2030 and to zero by 2050—is daunting. Everything discussed here will move us much more quickly, but some fundamental changes are needed in how we think about products, services, and consumption. Current business models and delivery methods can lock us into more material- and energy-intensive pathways. And some sectors, the most carbon-intensive, will need to exit core businesses.

Consider Philips Lighting, which launched a "light as a service" model, through which business customers pay Philips to install and manage their lighting rather than purchase a lighting system themselves. This flips Philips's traditional model on its head: Instead of trying to sell as many bulbs as possible, under this program, the company manages the provision of light as frugally as it can, using longer-lasting, more-efficient products that slash material and energy use. In a larger-scale transformation, the energy company Ørsted—formerly known as Danish Oil & Natural Gas—anticipated the decarbonization of the global economy and began pivoting from its core business a decade ago. It has since sold off most of its fossil fuel assets and has become the world's largest builder of offshore wind farms. And just a few years ago, the idea that meat-based McDonald's and Burger King would both be selling plant-based "burgers" seemed far-fetched. But they, like Ørsted, may be thinking strategically about what the coming low-carbon economy means for their business.

The Next Level of Action

There's no doubt that companies are doing a lot on climate, including cutting emissions and setting aggressive carbon goals for operations, supply chains, and their innovation agendas. But it's not enough. The science is getting away from us, and we're losing the relatively stable planetary temperature range that allowed us to build our society over the past 10,000 years. Companies have many levers to pull to truly change business as usual, but most remain stuck in old thinking. Climate action is usually focused on incremental change. And even when they're setting a big goal like going to all-renewable energy, companies have waited until every project makes money quickly. Now they need to mobilize *all* corporate assets, hard *and* soft, to tackle this shared, unprecedented problem at the scale it requires.

Next-gen climate actions, as they become an expected part of business, will create significant long-term value. They will help companies build closer, lasting connections with key stakeholders; create clear and consistent regulatory environments that enable more sustainable practices that lower costs; and drive deeper, more-disruptive (or what I call *heretical*) innovation. Throw in the substantial intangible value—employee attraction and loyalty, lowered risk in supply chain, resilience, license to operate, societal relevance, and preparation for a very different future—and you have a powerful business case.

But it's also well past time to recognize that aggressive climate action is necessary if humanity is to survive and thrive. Business and society won't succeed unless and until we do all we can to tackle climate change.

———————

Your Company's Next Leader on Climate Is . . . the CFO

by Laura Palmeiro and Delphine Gibassier

If your chief financial officer is the last person you would think of to take charge on climate change, think again. Today, smart organizations are shifting their sustainability responsibilities toward the finance function.

There are several reasons for this change. First is the basic math, which falls largely within a CFO's purview. Mitigating and adapting to climate change will require close to $1 trillion in investments per year through 2030 for the economy as a whole, and is also expected to put at risk between $4.2 trillion and $43 trillion of tradable stock exchange assets by the end of the century, depending on the level of planetary warming. (The latter number is for a world that has warmed by 6 degrees Celsius.)

Second, cutting greenhouse gas (GHG) emissions leads to cost savings. If you cut emissions, you cut energy, which is a massive organizational cost—something CFOs pay close attention to. Third, because investors are pushing to make climate-safe investments, they want climate risks to be integrated within corporate financial disclosures. Finally, the business opportunities for climate change solutions are blooming. According to Chartered Professional Accountants of Canada, "As creators, enablers, preservers and reporters of sustainable value, accountants can make their organizations' adaptation efforts more effective." Taken together, these shifts are leading finance teams to include what were formerly called "nonfinancials" in their daily jobs.

CFO leadership on climate change is starting to pay off. For example, Adnams, a British brewery, recently saw an increase in the base cost of beer because hot summers were affecting barley production. To solve the problem, the CFO was able to offset these higher costs by looking at energy and water savings. The CFO of Mars, Claus Aagaard, has talked about how the company's sustainability plan allowed it to capitalize on cost savings within two years.

Through our research, our corporate experience at Danone, and our work with the UN Global Compact, we have determined four key ways in which sustainability is being centralized in the finance function—ways every corporate leader should be aware of.

Financial Tools Are Becoming More Green

Increasingly, we've seen finance teams greening more of their tools. What does this look like? Companies such as SSE or the Coca-Cola Hellenic Bottling Company, for example, have implemented "green CAPEX [capital expenditure]" systems. These structures, which involve small changes in investment decisions (like including an internal price on carbon emissions or loosening the payback period for investment decisions), have allowed climate change–friendly investments to take place on a larger scale.

Even more significant, Microsoft now has an internal carbon market codesigned by the finance and sustainability teams. Thanks to a carbon fee paid by subsidiaries based on the level of their GHG emissions—incentivizing them to cut their emissions—Microsoft has a carbon fund that fuels climate change–related investments, allowing more significant and global investments to be made. On January 16, 2020, Microsoft made a historic announcement, backed by its CFO, to become carbon negative by 2030 and remove their historical carbon emissions by 2050.

In fact, more than 600 organizations say they now use carbon pricing, for a number of different reasons, among them to inform procurement and R&D decisions, help suppliers transition to a low-carbon world, pay bonuses, or help with long-term investments. In another change, Danone has started rewarding strong group performance by connecting incentives to climate change performance based on annual CDP scores.

Finally, following the integration of climate change within management control systems, corporations have started to measure GHG emissions like they measure their financials. Oracle has used what it calls "environmental accounting and reporting" to capture and transform GHG emissions from the company's portfolio of 600 buildings across more than 70 countries. This has led to significant cost savings, because accurate data is being collected quickly. Even the small French company Saveurs et Vie, which produces food baskets for the elderly, has asked its enterprise resource planning system provider to allow it to automate carbon footprinting.

Finance Teams, Collaborations, and Roles Are Evolving

Changes in finance and accounting departments are increasingly visible within not only the tools but also the teams. Ørsted, a wind-power company based in Denmark, has a full-time environmental, social, and governance (ESG) accounting team made up of four employees. The UK-based energy provider SSE has a full-time sustainability accountant in-house. Since 2013, Unilever has had a finance director for sustainability, who is in charge of developing an understanding of sustainability in finance, integrating sustainability into finance reporting, and developing best practices.

These company-specific examples are giving way to larger collaborations, too. The CFO Leadership Network, created in 2010 by Accounting for Sustainability in the UK, recently developed two Canadian and U.S. charters.

Some are rethinking the traditional CFO role altogether. In 2018, the Institute of Management Accountants published the first study on the emergence of sustainability CFOs (coauthored by one of us, Delphine), demonstrating the need for specific hybridized competencies between finance and sustainability to answer today's challenges. This research uncovered new competencies these leaders need to have, including developing natural capital profit and loss accounts, identifying the cost of key externalities, and understanding the value created through intangibles. Going further, Mervyn King (who is credited with the birth of "integrated reporting" in South Africa) developed the concept of a chief value officer in a 2016 book. And in North America, Manulife brought on a sustainability accounting director as a new kind of role.

Rules and Regulations Are Changing Rapidly

Your CFO will also need to adapt to shifting financial accounting rules that address climate change–related risks and opportunities. The biggest changes stem from December 2015, when the Financial Stability Board, an international body that monitors and makes recommendations about the global financial system, established the Task Force on Climate-related Financial Disclosures (TCFD) "to develop a set of voluntary, consistent disclosure recommendations for use by companies in providing information to investors, lenders and insurance underwriters about their climate-related financial risks." The new TCFD recommendations were released in June 2017 and included the suggestion that climate-related financial disclosures be made within mainstream annual financial filings and under governance processes similar to those for public disclosures.

What does this mean in practice? For one, all disclosures, including climate-related risks, climate metrics, and targets, should be reviewed by a company's CFO, audit committee, or both. Companies also should face the future risks of their business models through scenario analysis.

In November 2019, the International Accounting Standards Board (IASB), whose mission is to develop accounting standards for financial markets around the world, published the report "IFRS Standards and Climate-Related Disclosures," which recommended that companies address material environmental and societal issues and, more specifically, issues driven by investor pressure to disclose climate-related risks. (This was especially significant because the IASB usually does not mention climate change in accounting standards or briefings.) We expect recommendations like those from the TCFD and the IASB to continue.

The Financial Markets Increasingly Require a Focus on Climate

The financial markets are driving CFOs to look seriously at climate change. For example, the investor initiative Climate Action 100+, representing more than 370 investors with over $35 trillion in assets collectively, is urging 100 systemically important emitters to curb emissions, improve governance, and strengthen climate-related financial disclosures. Other initiatives, such as the climate benchmarks published by the European Union or the UN's Net Zero Asset Owner Alliance, are shifting the investment world into climate-ready financing. And in his annual letter to CEOs, BlackRock's Larry Fink emphasized that "the evidence on climate risk is compelling investors to reassess core assumptions about modern finance." Ultimately, Fink concluded that "climate risk is investment risk" and is alerting clients that BlackRock is centering its investment approach around sustainability.

Another reason for CFOs to take climate seriously comes from investors' appetite for green bonds—bonds that enable capital raising and investment for new and existing projects with environmental benefits. In 2019, new issuances on the green bond market reached around $250 billion overall, channeling more and more investments toward fighting climate change. Within this market, certified climate bonds, which are verified according to the type of physical asset or infrastructure they fund, allow companies to precisely align themselves with the 2015 Paris Agreement because they are consistent with its warming limit of 2 degrees Celsius. In addition to enabling the financing of environmental projects, these instruments may even represent an advantage in terms of cost of capital, since external financing can, in some cases, become indexed on ESG performance.

When Peter Bakker from the World Business Council for Sustainable Development said in 2012 that "accountants would save the planet," he was not far from the truth. Today, accountants are increasingly prioritizing climate change inside their organizations and beyond. Your CFO should be the next leader to follow.

A Better Way to Talk about the Climate Crisis

by Gretchen Gavett

Many of us care about the climate, but it can be challenging to talk about. It's easy to get bogged down in stats and statistics, for one. And it can be nerve-racking to approach someone if you don't already know what their beliefs on the topic are. Sometimes, it's easier to just keep our mouths shut.

Given the urgency of the climate crisis, however, many of us feel that silence is no longer an option. And Dr. Katharine Hayhoe, a climate scientist at Texas Tech University, is the person to talk to about how to talk about climate change. Hayhoe, whose 2018 TEDWomen talk on the subject has been viewed almost 2 million times, talks to everyone about the topic: Uber drivers, church ladies, Rotary Club members, business leaders, managers, elected officials, and more. People may have different backgrounds and views, but she's found a strategy that works: focusing on the heart—that is, what we collectively value—as opposed to the head.

So no matter your conversational goal, whether it's encouraging your company to act on climate issues or getting your employees to understand how the decisions they make affect your company's climate goals, this edited interview with Dr. Hayhoe is a great place to start.

What should any leader take into consideration when talking to people—employees, clients, suppliers, etc.—about climate change?

Ultimately, whether you're training a new employee, reviewing best practices with a supplier, or just having a conversation about climate change with a client, follow this rule of thumb: Don't start with fear, judgment, condemnation, or guilt. And don't start with just overwhelming people with facts and figures. *Do* start by connecting the dots to what is already important to both of us, and then offer positive, beneficial, and practical solutions that we can engage in.

Why have you found that this method works best? And how does it lead people toward understanding the urgency of climate change and taking action?

Often we believe that to care about climate change we have to be a certain type of person: an environmentalist, someone who bikes to work, or is a vegan. And if we're not any of those things, then we think, "Why should climate change matter to me?" But the reality is that if we are a human living on planet Earth, then climate change already matters to every single one of us; we just haven't realized it yet. Why? Because climate change affects the economy, the availability of natural resources, prices, jobs, international competition, and more. Failing to account for climate change in future long-range planning could lose us a competitive edge even in a best-case scenario, and potentially mean the end of a product line or an entire business in the worst case. By connecting climate impacts to what we already care about, we can recognize the importance and urgency of taking action.

So if I'm a leader, what are some specific ways in which I can communicate with my employees that sustainability is a key part of their jobs?

I would start early. During their initial training, I would explain very clearly how our products, our production, and our waste contributes to the problem of climate change. If our production is very energy intensive or produces a lot of organic waste, for example, that means we may be generating massive amounts of greenhouse gases. If our goods are transported over long distances, that also requires fossil fuels that produce heat-trapping gases. And aside from the issue of climate change, if we produce a lot of nonrecyclable waste that just piles up in landfills or the ocean, how much are we contributing to the pollution problem as well?

But I would also be sure to pair this information hand in hand with what we're doing to fix the problems from our end and how it's paying off. Give people analogies so it's really clear, so they can see it. I love giving examples of how many X worth of Y we've reduced; for example, something like "Through increasing the energy efficiency of our facilities, we have taken the equivalent of 500 cars off the road. Isn't that incredible? That's what we've been doing through our efforts." Or, "We have reduced our waste by 50%. That's the equivalent of X garbage trucks of waste per year." Or, "We are now powered by 38 wind turbines; that's X trainloads of coal we don't need to use anymore."

Finally—and this is the most important part!—I'd engage the employees themselves in the solutions. As humans, we want to be part of a solution. We want to make a difference. That is part of what gives us hope and what gives us energy, the idea that we're actually doing something good for the world.

So, for example, I might say, "We're aiming for an even better milestone. I want your ideas to help us get to this new milestone, too." That's even more incentivizing, when you feel like a company encourages you and supports you and wants you to be part of their plan.

Does this advice extend to people who might not believe that climate change is that severe—or that it exists at all? What might this kind of conversation look like in a professional setting?

Only around 10% of the population is dismissive [of climate change], but they are a very loud 10%. Glance at the comment section of any online article on climate change, check out the responses to my tweets, or search for global warming videos on YouTube—they're everywhere. They're even at our Thanksgiving dinner, because just about every one of us has at least one person who is dismissive in the family. I do, too!

A person who is dismissive is someone who has built their identity on rejecting the reality of a changing climate because they believe the solutions represent a direct and immediate threat to all they hold dear. And in pursuit of that goal, they will reject anything: hundreds of scientific studies, thousands of experts, even the evidence of their own eyes. So, no, there is no point talking to a dismissive about climate science or impacts, unless you enjoy banging your head against the wall.

But it *can* be possible to have a constructive conversation with a dismissive—and I've had these!—by focusing solely on solutions that they don't see as a threat because they carry positive benefits and/or are good for their bottom line. And the fascinating thing is that once they are engaged in helping fix the problem, that very action can have the power to change a dismissive person's mind.

I want to end by asking about the importance of climate conversation over the next few years. I've heard anecdotally that companies are hearing more questions from younger job candidates or employees: "What are you doing? How are you addressing climate change as a company?" Does that resonate with you at all? Should companies be preparing for more conversations like these?

We see a very strong age gradient when it comes to levels of concern about climate change primarily among conservative populations, with younger people caring much more and being much more engaged than their elders. (Among more liberal populations, levels of concern are relatively high across all age groups.) At my own school, the number of students going to the president and asking, "What is our university doing?" has increased noticeably. I hear this anecdotally from colleagues all around the country, too. And when those students graduate, that's what they ask in their interviews, because they want to be part of the solution. Young people understand how urgent the problem is, and they know that there's no time to waste. A lot of them don't want to do a job that is not helping to fix this massive problem that we have.

If companies want to be competitive, if they want to hire the best and the brightest, the ones who are most engaged, the ones who are most in tune, the ones who really put their heart and their soul and their passion into their work, then they have to start talking about climate change differently. Because this is increasingly becoming something that young professionals really care about.

Originally published in January 2020. Reprint BG2001

That Discomfort You're Feeling Is Grief

by Scott Berinato

SOME OF THE HBR EDIT STAFF met virtually the other day—a screen full of faces in a scene becoming more common everywhere. We talked about the content we're commissioning in this harrowing time of a pandemic and how we can help people. But we also talked about how we were feeling. One colleague mentioned that what she felt was grief. Heads nodded in all the panes.

If we can name it, perhaps we can manage it. We turned to David Kessler for ideas on how to do that. Kessler is the world's foremost expert on grief. He cowrote with Elisabeth Kübler-Ross *On Grief and Grieving: Finding the Meaning of Grief through the Five Stages of Loss.* His new book adds another stage to the process, *Finding Meaning: The Sixth Stage of Grief.* Kessler also has worked for a decade in a three-hospital system in Los Angeles. He served on their biohazards team. His volunteer work includes being an LAPD Specialist Reserve for traumatic events as well as having served on the Red Cross's disaster services team. He is the founder of www.grief.com, which has over 5 million visits yearly from 167 countries.

Kessler shared his thoughts on why it's important to acknowledge the grief you may be feeling, how to manage it, and how he believes we will find meaning in it. The conversation is lightly edited for clarity.

People are feeling any number of things right now. Is it right to call some of what they're feeling grief?

Yes, and we're feeling a number of different griefs. We feel the world has changed, and it has. We know this is temporary, but it doesn't feel that way, and we realize things will be different. Just as going to the airport is forever different from how it was before 9/11, things will change and this is the point at which they changed. The loss of normalcy; the fear of economic toll; the loss of connection. This is hitting us and we're grieving. Collectively. We are not used to this kind of collective grief in the air.

You said we're feeling more than one kind of grief?

Yes, we're also feeling anticipatory grief. Anticipatory grief is that feeling we get about what the future holds when we're uncertain. Usually it centers on death. We feel it when someone gets a dire diagnosis or when we have the normal thought that we'll lose a parent someday. Anticipatory grief is also more broadly imagined futures. There is a storm coming. There's something bad out there. With a virus, this kind of grief is so confusing for people. Our primitive mind knows something bad is happening, but you can't see it. This breaks our sense of safety. We're feeling that loss of safety. I don't think we've collectively lost our sense of general safety like this. Individually or as smaller groups, people have felt this. But all together, this is new. We are grieving on a micro and a macro level.

What can individuals do to manage all this grief?

Understanding the stages of grief is a start. But whenever I talk about the stages of grief, I have to remind people that the stages aren't linear and may not happen in this order. It's not a map, but it provides some scaffolding for this unknown world. There's denial, which we say a lot of early on: *This virus won't affect us.* There's anger: *You're making me stay home and taking away my activities.* There's bargaining: *Okay, if I social distance for two weeks, everything will be better, right?* There's sadness: *I don't know when this will end.* And finally there's acceptance. *This is happening; I have to figure out how to proceed.*

Idea in Brief

During the global pandemic, a palpable sense of collective grief has emerged. In an interview with HBR, grief expert David Kessler explains the classic five stages of grief and the practical steps we can take to manage these emotions throughout the crisis. These include balancing bad thoughts with good; focusing on the present; letting go of things you can't control; and stocking up on compassion. Kessler also talks about a sixth stage of grief: meaning. After acceptance, he says, we will find meaning in the hard-to-fathom events, and we will be stronger for it.

Acceptance, as you might imagine, is where the power lies. We find control in acceptance. *I can wash my hands. I can keep a safe distance. I can learn how to work virtually.*

When we're feeling grief, there's that physical pain. And the racing mind. Are there techniques to deal with that to make it less intense?

Let's go back to anticipatory grief. Unhealthy anticipatory grief is really anxiety, and that's the feeling you're talking about. Our mind begins to show us images. My parents getting sick. We see the worst scenarios. That's our minds being protective. Our goal is not to ignore those images or to try to make them go away—your mind won't let you do that, and it can be painful to try and force it. The goal is to **find balance in the things you're thinking**. If you feel the worst image taking shape, make yourself think of the best image. We all get a little sick and the world continues. Not everyone I love dies. Maybe no one does because we're all taking the right steps. Neither scenario should be ignored, but neither should dominate either.

Anticipatory grief is the mind going to the future and imagining the worst. To calm yourself, you want to **come into the present**. This will be familiar advice to anyone who has meditated or practiced mindfulness, but people are always surprised at how prosaic this can be. You can name five things in the room. There's a computer, a chair, a picture of the dog, an old rug, and a coffee mug. It's that simple. Breathe. Realize that in the present moment, nothing you've anticipated has happened. In this moment, you're okay. You have food. You are not sick. Use your senses and think about what they feel. The desk is hard. The blanket is soft. I can feel the breath coming into my nose. This really will work to dampen some of that pain. You can also think about how to **let go of what you can't control.** What your neighbor is doing is out of your control. What is in your control is staying six feet away from them and washing your hands. Focus on that.

Finally, it's a good time to **stock up on compassion.** Everyone will have different levels of fear and grief, and it manifests in different ways. A coworker got very snippy with me the other day, and I thought, *That's not like this person; that's how they're dealing with this. I'm seeing their fear and anxiety.* So be patient. Think about who someone usually is and not who they seem to be in this moment.

One particularly troubling aspect of this pandemic is the open-endedness of it.

This is a temporary state. It helps to say it. I worked for 10 years in the hospital system. I've been trained for situations like this. I've also studied the 1918 flu pandemic. The precautions we're taking are the right ones. History tells us that. This is survivable. We will survive. This is a time to overprotect but not overreact.

And, I believe we will find meaning in it. I've been honored that Elisabeth Kübler-Ross's family has given me permission to add a sixth stage to grief: meaning. I had talked to Elisabeth quite a bit about what came after acceptance. I did not want to stop at acceptance when I experienced some personal grief. I wanted meaning in those darkest hours. And I do believe we find light in those times. Even now people are realizing they can connect through technology. They are not as remote as they thought. They are realizing they can use their phones for long conversations. They're appreciating walks. I believe we will continue to find meaning now and when this is over.

What do you say to someone who's read all this and is still feeling overwhelmed with grief?

Keep trying. There is something powerful about naming this as grief. It helps us feel what's inside of us. So many have told me in the past week, "I'm telling my coworkers I'm having a hard time," or "I cried last night." When you name it, you feel it and it moves through you. Emotions need motion. It's important we acknowledge what we go through. One unfortunate by-product of the self-help movement is we're the first generation to have feelings about our feelings. We tell ourselves things like, *I feel sad, but I shouldn't feel that; other people have it worse.* We can—we should—stop at the first feeling. *I feel sad. Let me go for five minutes to feel sad.* Your work is to feel your sadness and fear and anger whether or not someone else is feeling something. Fighting it doesn't help because your body is producing the feeling. If we allow the feelings to happen, they'll happen in an orderly way, and it empowers us. Then we're not victims.

In an orderly way?

Yes. Sometimes we try not to feel what we're feeling because we have this image of a "gang of feelings." If I feel sad and let that in, it'll never go away. The gang of bad feelings will overrun me. The truth is a feeling that moves through us. We feel it and it goes and then we go to the next feeling. There's no gang out to get us. It's absurd to think we shouldn't feel grief right now. Let yourself feel the grief and keep going.

Originally published in March 2020. Reprint H05HVE

About the Contributors

SCOTT BERINATO is a senior editor at *Harvard Business Review* and the author of *Good Charts Workbook: Tips, Tools, and Exercises for Making Better Data Visualizations* (Harvard Business Review Press, 2019) and *Good Charts: The HBR Guide to Making Smarter, More Persuasive Data Visualizations* (Harvard Business Review Press, 2016).

MARCUS BUCKINGHAM is the head of people and performance research at the ADP Research Institute. He is a coauthor of *Nine Lies about Work: A Freethinking Leader's Guide to the Real World* (Harvard Business Review Press, 2019).

PETER CAPPELLI is the George W. Taylor Professor of Management at the Wharton School and the director of its Center for Human Resources. His most recent book is *Will College Pay Off? A Guide to the Most Important Financial Decision You'll Ever Make* (Public-Affairs, 2015).

TIZIANA CASCIARO is a professor of organizational behavior at the University of Toronto's Rotman School of Management.

PAIGE COHEN is an associate editor at *Harvard Business Review*.

AMY C. EDMONDSON is the Novartis Professor of Leadership and Management at Harvard Business School and author of *The Fearless Organization* (Wiley, 2019).

TIM FOUNTAINE is a partner in McKinsey's Sydney office and leads QuantumBlack, an advanced analytics firm owned by McKinsey, in Australia.

GRETCHEN GAVETT is a senior editor at *Harvard Business Review*.

DELPHINE GIBASSIER is an associate professor of accounting for sustainable development at Audencia Business School, with 18 years of experience in financial and nonfinancial accounting. She holds a PhD from HEC Paris.

ASHLEY GOODALL is the senior vice president of leadership and team intelligence at Cisco Systems. He is a coauthor of *Nine Lies about Work: A Freethinking Leader's Guide to the Real World* (Harvard Business Review Press, 2019).

ANDREI HAGIU is an associate professor of information systems at Boston University's Questrom School of Business. Twitter: @theplatformguy.

DANE E. HOLMES is the global head of human capital management at Goldman Sachs.

SUJIN JANG is an assistant professor of organizational behavior at INSEAD.

ANTHONY J. MAYO is the Thomas S. Murphy Senior Lecturer of Business Administration in the Organizational Behavior Unit at Harvard Business School. With Laura Morgan Roberts and Morehouse College president David A. Thomas, he edited *Race, Work, and Leadership: New Perspectives on the Black Experience* (Harvard Business Review Press, 2019), an exploration of the resources and actions needed for organizations to eliminate systemic racism.

BRIAN MCCARTHY is a partner in McKinsey's Atlanta office and coleads the knowledge development agenda for McKinsey Analytics.

LAURA PALMEIRO is the senior adviser to the United Nations Global Compact. She has extensive experience in finance, controlling, and sustainability at PwC and Danone. She holds an MBA from IAE Argentina.

JENNIFER PETRIGLIERI is an associate professor of organizational behavior at INSEAD and the author of *Couples That Work: How Dual-Career Couples Can Thrive in Love and Work* (Harvard Business Review Press, 2019). At INSEAD she directs the Management

Acceleration Programme, the Women Leaders Programme, and the Gender Diversity Programme.

GARY P. PISANO is the Harry E. Figgie Jr. Professor of Business Administration and the senior associate dean of faculty development at Harvard Business School. He is the author of *Creative Construction: The DNA of Sustained Innovation* (PublicAffairs, 2019).

LAURA MORGAN ROBERTS is a professor of practice at the University of Virginia's Darden School of Business. With Anthony J. Mayo and Morehouse College president David A. Thomas, she edited *Race, Work, and Leadership: New Perspectives on the Black Experience* (Harvard Business Review Press, 2019), an exploration of the resources and actions needed for organizations to eliminate systemic racism.

TAMIM SALEH is a senior partner in McKinsey's London office and heads McKinsey Analytics in Europe.

KATINA B. SAWYER is an assistant professor of management at The George Washington University.

NICOLAJ SIGGELKOW is a professor of management and strategy at Wharton and a codirector of the Mack Institute for Innovation Management. He is a coauthor of *Connected Strategy: Building Continuous Customer Relationships for Competitive Advantage* (Harvard Business Review Press, 2019).

JANE STEVENSON, the global leader for CEO succession and vice chair of board and CEO services at Korn Ferry, is a coauthor of *Breaking Away: How Great Leaders Create Innovation That Drives Sustainable Growth—and Why Others Fail* (McGraw-Hill, 2011).

CHRISTIAN TERWIESCH is a professor of operations and innovation at Wharton and a codirector of the Mack Institute for Innovation Management. He is a coauthor of *Connected Strategy: Building*

Continuous Customer Relationships for Competitive Advantage (Harvard Business Review Press, 2019).

MELISSA THOMAS-HUNT holds a faculty appointment at Stanford Graduate School of Business and has worked in professorial roles for more than 20 years at schools such as Vanderbilt, University of Virginia, Cornell University, and Washington University in St. Louis. Her research and teaching has focused on organizational behavior and the factors that unleash, leverage, and amplify the talents and contributions made by women and underrepresented individuals. In May 2019, Dr. Thomas-Hunt joined Airbnb as head of global diversity and belonging. She serves on the company's executive team and leads the strategy and execution of the global internal diversity, inclusion, equity, and belonging programs.

CHRISTIAN N. THOROUGHGOOD is an assistant professor of psychology in the Department of Psychological and Brain Sciences and the graduate programs in human resource development at Villanova University.

JENNICA R. WEBSTER is a codirector of the Institute for Women's Leadership and an associate professor of management at Marquette University.

ANDREW WINSTON is the founder of Winston Eco-Strategies and a global expert on business and sustainability. He is the author of *The Big Pivot: Radically Practical Strategies for a Hotter, Scarcer, and More Open World* (Harvard Business Review Press, 2014).

JULIAN WRIGHT is a professor of economics at the National University of Singapore.

Index

Engage with HBR content the way you want, on any device.

With HBR's new subscription plans, you can access world-renowned **case studies** from Harvard Business School and receive **four free eBooks**. Download and customize prebuilt **slide decks and graphics** from our **Visual Library**. With HBR's archive, top 50 best-selling articles, and five new articles every day, HBR is more than just a magazine.

Subscribe Today
hbr.org/success

The most important management ideas all in one place.

We hope you enjoyed this book from *Harvard Business Review*. Now you can get even more with HBR's 10 Must Reads Boxed Set. From books on leadership and strategy to managing yourself and others, this 6-book collection delivers articles on the most essential business topics to help you succeed.

HBR's 10 Must Reads Series

The definitive collection of ideas and best practices on our most sought-after topics from the best minds in business.

- Change Management
- Collaboration
- Communication
- Emotional Intelligence
- Innovation
- Leadership
- Making Smart Decisions

- Managing Across Cultures
- Managing People
- Managing Yourself
- Strategic Marketing
- Strategy
- Teams
- The Essentials

hbr.org/mustreads

Buy for your team, clients, or event.
Visit hbr.org/bulksales for quantity discount rates.